# FOUNDATIONS
# OF THE METAPHYSICS
# OF MORALS

The Library of Liberal Arts

OSKAR PIEST, FOUNDER

# FOUNDATIONS
# OF THE METAPHYSICS
# OF MORALS

*and*

## WHAT IS ENLIGHTENMENT?

## IMMANUEL KANT

Translated, with an Introduction, by
LEWIS WHITE BECK,

The Library of Liberal Arts
*published by*
**Bobbs-Merrill Educational Publishing**
**Indianapolis**

**Immanuel Kant: 1724-1804**

GRUNDLEGUNG ZUR METAPHYSIK DER SITTEN

was originally published in 1785

Copyright © 1959 by The Bobbs-Merrill Company, Inc.
Printed in the United States of America

The Bobbs-Merrill Company, Inc.
4300 West 62nd Street
Indianapolis, Indiana 46268


Twenty-first Printing—1980
Library of Congress Catalog Card Number 59–11679
ISBN 0–672–60312–8 (pbk.)
ISBN 0–672–51047–2

# CONTENTS

· · · · · · · · · · · · · · · ·

## I. FOUNDATIONS OF THE METAPHYSICS OF MORALS

## II. WHAT IS ENLIGHTENMENT?

# INTRODUCTION

## I

*Grundlegung zur Metaphysik der Sitten,* published in 1785, is one of the most important ethical treatises ever written. Unlike Kant's other great ethical works, it does not presuppose any knowledge of his *Critique of Pure Reason,* and it is a vivid refutation of the common view that Kant is always obscure, dry, and difficult. For these reasons it is an eminently suitable introduction to moral philosophy and to the philosophy of Kant as a whole. But unlike some introductions, it is not a work to be read and then put aside for weightier things; like all classics it reveals more on each reading, and Professor Paton has called it "one of the small books which are truly great: it has exercised on human thought an influence almost ludicrously disproportionate to its size." [1]

The *Foundations* is for the general reader who possesses "common rational knowledge of morality" but lacks a philosophical theory of it. The ordinary man knows very well in most cases what he ought to do, but he may not be able to defend his views against criticism. Hence Kant begins with the commonly held Christian-humanistic ideals of Western civilization, and examines them to determine their presuppositions so that he can construct a system of moral precepts which can be intellectually defended.

We must take the title of the book very literally. It is a study of *foundations,* not a construction of a system. Kant is not writing casuistry, wherein each duty and privilege is delineated; he is looking for the "axioms" which might be used in erecting a general system of laws. Metaphysics, as Kant uses this word here, is not speculation concerning "ulti-

---

[1] H. J. Paton, in the Preface to his translation of the *Foundations,* published as *The Moral Law, or Kant's Groundwork of the Metaphysics of Morals* (London, 1949).

mate reality," but a rigorous study of certain laws (such as that of "duty") which, unlike the laws of psychology, cannot be derived from observation of men's actual behavior but require to be established by reason. In the light of the fifth paragraph of the Preface we might paraphrase the title of the work: it could well be called *Foundations of Ethics Based on Reason.*

Kant says, in the opening sentence of the First Section, that there is nothing in or out of the world (i.e., nothing either human or divine) that is absolutely good except a good will. However much men may desire happiness and value traits of character and the gifts of fortune which help them in their search for happiness, they do not attribute to happiness and to skill in attaining it an *absolute* value; the "rational impartial observer" cannot approve of "a being adorned with no feature of a pure and good will yet enjoying uninterrupted prosperity." Though being good is not the cause of happiness —happiness depends not only on character but also on circumstances—it is a condition of *worthiness* to be happy. This belief expressed here by Kant is an essential part of the Platonic, Stoic, and Christian traditions. The care of one's soul and the striving for "purity of heart" are absolute obligations of man; if it is true that "all these things will be added unto you" they will indeed be very gladly received—but that they come is not a part of the man's responsibility once he has earnestly sought the "kingdom of God" or—for Kant—the possession of a good will.

The common man is very well aware of the difference between being good and being clever, and though men by nature desire to be happy, they do not ordinarily think that morality is merely a means to happiness (though they may think that being moral is likely in the long run to lead to it). It is sometimes said that Kant believed that a moral act cannot be an act we want to do, and that in acting morally we ought to take no account of consequences. But he is insisting merely that in deciding what we *ought* to do our variable desires are irrelevant. Kant is neither an ascetic nor a pharisaical formalist. He is, I believe, describing the "common moral consciousness." To see how his view of the good will fits "common sense morality," consider an example.

Imagine two soldiers who volunteer for a dangerous mission; because they see a task they ought to undertake, they voluntarily assume the responsibility for it. Certainly their act will have consequences; equally certain is the fact that they desire certain consequences for their act. The most careful consideration of these consequences, calculation as to how to achieve some desirable consequences and avoid others less desirable, and an ardent desire to attain the goal do not in the least detract from the morality of the men's action if they are indeed acting on the conviction that it is their duty to do these acts; their concern with the consequences may be an essential part of their conduct, necessary for the fulfillment of the obligation they have placed upon themselves. Now imagine that one of the men is killed before reaching his destination, while the other is successful; what moral judgment do we pass upon them? So far as we judge that their motives were equally good (and of course, as Kant repeatedly says, we cannot be sure what anyone's motives really are), we judge them in the same way. Their acts are judged to be equally moral, in spite of the fact that one succeeded and the other failed. Each did his "best," and what he earnestly attempted and the motives which led him to do what he did are the proper objects of moral judgment; what he accomplishes lies to a large extent beyond his control.

This example, simple as it is, contains the kernel of the argument of the First Section. Kant elicits from "common moral knowledge" the principles given on page 16. An action is not truly moral unless it is done in the belief and because of the belief that it is right, i.e.; out of respect for a moral law. It is not sufficient that it accord with a law but arise from some subjective, private, and variable inclination, no matter how "well disposed" the person's temperament may be.[2] Whether the action succeeds in its purpose or not, if it is done with a "good will" it is morally acceptable; the consequences which we consider in passing moral judgment are the *intended* consequences implicated in the motive of the action, not the actual consequences which no man can wholly foresee and control. Many actions are in accord with the law but are not yet moral (as, for example, the act of the soldier who volunteers merely to avoid some greater danger he foresees), for the motive to such lawful actions is not a "good will," a striving to do one's duty, but some prudential calculation as to what one will "get out of it." If an action is really moral, it will not only accord with a law; it will be done because a law is acknowledged as absolutely and universally binding.

These are the ruling ideas of Kant's ethics, on which, the poet Schiller says, "Only philosophers disagree, but men have always been unanimous." But this agreement is by no means agreement as to what the moral law prescribes in a specific case. The determination of what this law is and what it prescribes is a task of reason. Only pure reason can decide what is an absolutely universal law, permitting no exceptions. An analogy will make this clear.

We cannot have a science of geometry if we merely describe figures drawn on a blackboard; for then we could not say, "*All* triangles have the sum of their internal angles equal to two right angles." Yet we can say this, without measuring all

[2] Lest it be thought that this view is peculiar to Kant, consider the opinion of Samuel Johnson, no philosopher but a man of sound moral judgment and common sense. Boswell writes: " 'Sir,' said Mr. Johnson, 'I can lay but little stress upon that instinctive, that constitutional, goodness that is not founded upon principle. I grant you that such a man may be a very good member of society. I can conceive him placed in such a situation that he is not much tempted to deviate from what is right; and so, as goodness is most eligible when there is not some strong enticement to transgress its precepts, I can conceive him doing no harm. But if such a man stood in need of money, I should not like to trust him. And even now, I should not trust Mr. Dempster with young ladies, for there is always temptation.' " (*London Journal*, 22 July 1763; a similar account is given in *The Life of Samuel Johnson* [Modern Library edition, p. 268].)

triangles. Similarly, we could not say, as we do, *"All* men ought in *all.* cases to treat human beings as ends in themselves," if ethics were merely a descriptive science of how human beings actually feel and behave. Yet we do, both in ethics and in ordinary moral concern, enunciate such universal judgments. Just as geometry is a science with universal rules, so also ethics must be if there are absolutely binding moral laws. Since in neither case can these universal rules or laws be derived by induction, they must, Kant believes, come from some non-empirical activity of the mind, which he calls "pure reason." The system of such rules is what Kant calls "metaphysics," and "metaphysics of morals" will be the system of such rules of conduct; it will be, as we mentioned earlier, "ethics based on pure reason."

## II

The discovery of the foundations of the metaphysics of morals occupies Kant in the Second Section.[3] He tells us again, in the first ten paragraphs, why "pure ethics" cannot describe the way men actually behave, and here and in the closing paragraphs of the Section he criticizes other philosophers who have based their ethics on such description. The constructive part of the work is found in the intervening paragraphs, running from page 29 to page 60. We may divide the construction into five steps.

(1) The will is practical reason (p. 29). While all things in nature work "according to law," a rational being is one which can govern its behavior by a *conception* of law. "Will" is the name generally (and not merely by Kant) given to this ground or discipline of action. The principle to which we refer in governing our action is an imperative, an expression containing an "ought."

(2) An imperative is hypothetical (i.e., it has an "if-clause") if it states that some action is right or advisable as a means

[3] Actually the construction is begun, in a tentative way, in the First Section, p. 18.

to some specific goal. Such an imperative says, "If you would accomplish such and such a goal, you ought to do so and so." An imperative of this kind comes from our experience of the ways in which we may best satisfy our desires; it does not come from pure reason. Hence it does not "command," as a moral law does, but only "counsels" us to some line of action. For if the goal is some specific object of desire, the goal cannot be supposed to be universally held by all men or by myself at all times; hence the imperative is conditional upon circumstances and moods. Or if the goal is happiness, which we may correctly suppose is desired by all men, we still cannot formulate any universal hypothetical imperative, for "happiness" is a word of such variable meaning from man to man and from moment to moment that I cannot infer that all men should behave in the same way in order to attain it. Obviously, then, such hypothetical imperatives as we do make have not the status of peremptory and inexorable moral laws. If there is a binding moral law, as Kant believes, it cannot correspond to a hypothetical imperative.

(3) A moral imperative is unconditional, i.e., categorical. Such an imperative, which seems to be involved in the moral consciousness that we ought to do our duty regardless of our wayward inclinations, cannot, as we have seen, be derived from psychological study of what our inclinations and their goals are. If there is such an imperative, it must be formulated by pure reason. If, as in the case before us, no specific goal or "condition" is stated under which an action is obligatory, we must find a "formula of the 'ought'" from the mere concept of "ought" (p. 38). That is, the idea of obligation itself must dictate a criterion for deciding what our obligations are.

A moral imperative commands unconditional conformity of our subjective maxim to a law, while the law contains no condition, i.e., no reference to specific goals on which it depends. The rule for the maxim is that, if moral, it should contain no condition which would prevent it from being *itself* a law. But no maxim can be a moral law unless it could be universally imperative, i.e., valid for all men as rational beings regardless of their specific desires. Thus we have a test for deciding whether a maxim is admissible or not: is it a maxim which a rational being could consistently will to be a maxim for all rational beings? The categorical imperative—"Act only according to that maxim by which you can at the same time will that it should become a universal law"—is the criterion for deciding whether a maxim is moral.

(4) There follows a derivation of other formulae of this imperative. The first (p. 39) requires that the maxim be fit to be a law of nature, where nature is considered as a harmonious, organic whole. The second (p. 47) is based on the notion that all actions have ends. Are there any ends which we ought to set before ourselves as valid for ourselves and for all men, regardless of specific personal aims? The answer is that man is an end in himself, and no maxim which does not respect man can be a moral law valid for all men. The third (p. 50) requires that we should act only in harmony with the idea of the will of every rational being as making universal laws. The fourth (p. 57) requires that the moral agent act as if he were a lawgiving member of a realm of ends, i.e., of persons, each of whom is an end in himself and an end for all others. These are said to be only different formulations of one and the same imperative.

(5) From these formulae, there arise two important conceptions: the autonomy of the will and the dignity of man (pp. 51, 54). In all previous attempts to discover the moral law, it was assumed that there had to be some *quid pro quo* for morality; hence all imperatives were regarded as hypothetical and every man as having his "price." But the moral law can obligate unconditionally only if it is a law given by man as sovereign in the "realm of ends" to himself as a subject in this realm. In this conception man has the dignity of a lawgiver, and does not have to be bribed by fear of punishment or hope of reward into obedience to a law; the laws he obeys are the laws he gives himself. A being which gives the law to himself

is not merely bound to the law, but freely bound by his own lawgiving activity.[4] This is what Kant means by calling the moral law *autonomous*. A being which takes the law from some other lawgiver (God, a tyrant, his own cupidity, etc.) must be led to obedience by hope or fear; he is not free but *heteronomous*. He is not truly moral, because all his maxims are hypothetical, and he cannot act out of respect for a universal law which takes no account of the contingent and divisive interests of individuals.

## III

In spite of its title, the Third Section deals with questions which are likely nowadays to be considered "metaphysical." Heretofore, Kant's question has been: "What is morality, such that we could say, 'An action having such and such characters would be moral'?" This is very different from the new question, "Can such an action actually take place?" We cannot answer either question by citing examples; such questions must be answered by reason (p. 66, cf. p. 23).

The new question is whether the will of man is free. If it is not, morality is impossible, because in that case the will would be determined by something foreign to it and its imperatives would be hypothetical. To show that our "ethics based on reason" is more than a figment of the imagination, therefore, we must show that the will is free.

Since morality and autonomy, as we have just seen, are cognate or correlative concepts (i.e., concepts mutually implicative of each other, like "husband" and "wife"), we cannot use the *concept* of one to establish the *reality* of the other. Any argument that "we must be free because we are morally obligated" is a *petitio principii*, since "morally obligated" means "subject to a categorical imperative," and "free" means (in

---

[4] Kant does not, in this work, develop the political implications of this conception. But they are unmistakable even here, and have their full elaboration in *What Is Enlightenment?*, *Perpetual Peace*, and the *Metaphysics of Morals*.

this statement) autonomous, or "determined by no hypothetical imperative." [5]

To find a way out of this circle, Kant gives us, on pages 69 to 71, a rapid survey of some of the conclusions of the *Critique of Pure Reason* and the *Prolegomena to Any Future Metaphysics*. All that we perceive, he tells us, is only the appearances of things. These appearances are connected by causal laws and the system of them is "nature." We ourselves are parts of nature and hence under the laws of causal determination. But behind the appearances there is a real world we do not know, and behind the appearance of a man there is "something else as its basis, namely, his ego as it is in itself." Man ascribes to this ego whatever is "pure activity" in himself, for only this can be free from causal determination in the world of appearance. This pure activity is reason; hence as a reasonable being man may be presumed to be free, though as a sensuous being he is under the mechanism of nature.

In this way the Kantian theory of knowledge provides an escape from the vicious circle. It is shown, quite apart from moral considerations, that man can be "above nature" and thus free from its laws, while also a part of nature and as such not free. In his former role he gives a law to himself in his latter role. The categorical imperative expresses this constraint, while hypothetical imperatives express the force and attraction of inclinations in the world of sense.

Philosophy cannot establish any theoretical knowledge of this supersensible world in which we are citizens and lawgivers. Its task is to point out that freedom is possible and to mark out a region which fatalistic and materialistic speculations cannot successfully occupy so as to destroy the foundations of morality (p. 76). In the words of the *Critique of Pure Reason*, Kant has "found it necessary to deny knowledge

[5] The argument on p. 66 should be carefully examined. It shows that freedom must be presupposed *practically* even if it cannot be demonstrated theoretically. The rest of the argument does not indeed demonstrate freedom theoretically; but it shows that freedom is not merely *practically necessary* but *theoretically possible*.

[of the supersensible world] in order to make room for faith. The dogmatism of metaphysics . . . is the source of all that unbelief [in the presuppositions of morality], always very dogmatic, which wars against morality." [6] This, he tells us (p. 82) is the supreme limit of all moral inquiry.

## IV

I shall now consider a few common criticisms of Kant's ethics which are based on patent but widespread misinterpretations of his theory.

(1) *Kant's ethics is "empty," because the categorical imperative does not have any definite implications for action.* This reveals a misunderstanding of the function of the imperative. It is a rule like the rule of a syllogism, and just as the rules of a syllogism are empty but tell us what premises are logically necessary in drawing a specific conclusion, or what conclusions follow from given premises, the categorical imperative is a rule for determining what maxims are relevant in making a moral decision. The criticism assumes that the categorical imperative is a *premise* from which specific conclusions ought to be drawn; but no specific conclusions can be drawn from it any more than they can be drawn merely from the rules of the syllogism. In each case, premises or actual maxims have to be used, and the rules of logic and of ethics tell us which can be properly used or what their conclusion must be. The categorical imperative is not and was not meant to be a casuistical principle, or a motive, or an axiom from which moral decisions could be drawn as it were *in vacuo.*

(2) *Kant's ethics is trivial, and does not discriminate between moral and merely permissible actions.* For, it is said, I can make many maxims universal without rendering them moral. For instance, I have the policy of writing my name on the flyleaf of each of my books, and I can consistently will that all men, indeed all rational beings, should write their names

<hr />

[6] *Critique of Pure Reason,* Preface to second edition, p. xxx (translated by Norman Kemp Smith [London, 1923]), p. 29.

in their books; but this does not mean that I have a moral obligation to write my name in my books. This criticism, however, overlooks that fact that Kant carefully distinguishes between actions that conform to law (legal actions) and those done because of a law (moral actions). I do not write my name in my books because I can will that others should do so; I do so in order to keep them from getting lost. But in a moral action, I decide what I ought to do precisely by finding out what I will that every rational being should do. Kant does not, perhaps, make this as clear as one might wish. But he does assert that in moral action there are not two volitions (what I will directly, and what I will that others should will), but only one. The moral imperative is: "Never choose except in such a way that the maxims of the choice are comprehended *in the same volition* as a universal law" (p. 59; italics added). That is, I am obligated to do a moral action because I cannot consistently will that all rational beings should act in one way, and I in another.

(3) *Kant minimizes the role of practical intelligence in life, and instead of calling for more facts and acknowledging the problematic and tentative character of most of our difficult decisions, he requires us only to apply mechanically a simple logical rule.* On the contrary, Kant does not deny the need for facts in making decisions; but the question is, what facts are relevant if the decision is moral? How are we to decide, for instance, whether the color of a man's skin is a relevant fact in deciding whether he has certain rights? It is indeed one of the facts of the case, but we need a criterion to decide which facts are *morally* relevant. Modern legal and ethical philosophers, in their zeal to be open-minded, frequently are very vague on the question as to when we can safely ignore certain putative "facts of the case." Kant gives a rule for drawing a line: we must determine what a rational being could consistently take into account in his *willing*. The avoidance of formal logical contradiction is only a minor part of this rule, so to decide what can be consistently willed requires much more than a knowledge of formal logic.

(4) *Kant's theory is not "true to human nature"; Kant requires man to be more rational than he can be.* Certainly Kant is not an irrationalist; he does not believe that the reason is only a kind of "rationalization" of our emotions. He insists on the moral struggle which is necessary to bring our emotions under rational control; "Virtue," he says, "is the moral disposition in conflict." Kant insists that man is neither completely rational nor completely moral; but he also insists, in a way reminiscent of Aristotle and in many ways anticipating Dewey, that morality is conduct guided by reason. But reason is never claimed to be all-powerful, and Kant is, in fact, rather more pessimistic about man's rational competence than either Aristotle or Dewey.

(5) *Kant's ethics is one-sided because he despised the emotions.* This view arises from the fact that Kant is usually writing against philosophers who thought the emotions were primary and sufficient to morality, with the result that he emphasizes the prior role of reason and often seems to neglect the emotions. But if we read Kant with this polemical situation in mind, we can readily see why he did not *emphasize* the emotional though he was well aware of its place in conduct. Whenever the argument leads Kant naturally to recognize the role of the emotions, he readily does so without question and without inconsistency. In fact, he frequently discusses the emotional concomitants and expressions of virtues and vices and the culture of those emotions which favor the development of character.

The principal source of this misunderstanding is found in Kant's famous four examples, which he adduces again and again. These examples refer to men who have to go against their desires in order to do right, and they are often interpreted as evidence that Kant thought one cannot do right except when subduing his desires and going against his wishes. But this is not what the examples mean; they are not examples for emulation, but examples to elicit the moral element in action from a context in which there might be other values which would obscure its uniqueness. In all action there is some object of desire, and the satisfaction of some of these desires is often regarded as being the root of the moral value. So Kant devised examples in which the object of desire was in conflict with the moral motive, in order that the values of desire should not be confused with the moral value, which might then shine by contrast. Failure to understand the polemical reason for the singularly unattractive examples has led to misinterpretations of Kant as a proponent of sour virtue.[7]

(6) *Kant is "too rigoristic."* "Every 'law' has some exceptions," we are told, and Kant's denial that we should tell a lie even to save the life of an innocent person is taken as a *reductio ad absurdum* of his theory. Kant himself is to blame for this criticism, which is based on his own examples. Yet Kant is not, in principle, asserting the universality of any particular rule such as that against lying. Rather, the laws he insists upon are laws of *maxims,* not laws directly of *actions.* In view of this, the argument from "exceptions" takes on a very different appearance. The "exceptions" which are paraded by his critics are always exceptions to specific rules of actions; I do not believe that those who find "exceptions" mean to imply that "Sometimes it is moral to act from bad motives, i.e., sometimes we ought to be immoral." Yet only the latter would be an exception to the essential moral laws Kant attempts to establish.

(7) *Kant takes a "provincial moral code" and absolutizes it.* The same reply can be made to this as we made to (6). Certainly Kant's examples were taken from his and our tradition, but it is not the examples or the specific precepts which are universalized—though Kant, dealing with a highly homogeneous culture, never thought of the need to illustrate his doctrine with reference to examples taken from savage peoples. What is universalized is the requirement that a certain character be found in our rules regardless of their specific content, which will vary from man to man and culture to culture. He is thus in a better position than most "absolutists" to take

---

[7] Cf. my "Sir David Ross on Duty and Purpose in Kant," *Philosophy and Phenomenological Research,* XVI (1955), 99-107.

account of the facts of ethical relativity, for he has found, he believes, a principle of morality which is a cultural invariant. If he is successful in this search, he also has an answer to the skeptical conclusions usually drawn from cultural relativity, while at the same time he does not have to be ethnocentric by trying to establish a provincial code of specific rules as universally binding.

LEWIS WHITE BECK

# SKETCH OF KANT'S LIFE AND WORK

Immanuel Kant was born in Königsberg, East Prussia, April 22, 1724. His family were Pietists, a Protestant sect somewhat like the Quakers and early Methodists. Pietism's deeply ethical orientation and singular lack of emphasis on theological dogmatism became a part of Kant's nature and a determining factor in his philosophy. After attending the University of Königsberg and serving as tutor in several aristocratic families, Kant became an instructor at the university. He held this position for fifteen years, lecturing and writing on metaphysics, logic, ethics, and the natural sciences. In the sciences he made significant but, at the time, little recognized contributions, especially in physics, astronomy, geology, and meteorology.

In 1770 he was appointed Professor of Logic and Metaphysics at Königsberg, and in 1781 he published his most important work, the *Critique of Pure Reason.* This work opened up new fields of study and problems for him at an age when most men are ready to retire; but for Kant there followed a period of nearly twenty years of unremitting labor and unparalleled accomplishment. Merely a list of the most important writings shows this: *Prolegomena to Any Future Metaphysics* (1783); *Idea for a Universal History* (1784); *Fundamental Principles of the Metaphysics of Morals* (1785); *Metaphysical Foundations of Natural Science* (1786); second edition of *Critique of Pure Reason* (1787); *Critique of Practical Reason* (1787); *Critique of Judgment* (1790); *Religion within the Limits of Reason Alone* (1793); *Perpetual Peace* (1795); *Metaphysics of Ethics* (1797); *Anthropology from a Pragmatic Point of View* (1798). He died in Königsberg February 12, 1804.

Kant's personality, or at least a caricature of it, is well known. Most people who know nothing else of Kant do know that the housewives of Königsberg used to set their clocks by the regular afternoon walk he took, and that his life was said to pass like the most regular of regular verbs. But a truer picture of his personality—less pedantic, Prussian, and Puritanical—comes to us from the German writer Johann Gottfried Herder:

I have had the good fortune to know a philosopher. He was my teacher. In his prime he had the happy sprightliness of a youth; he continued to have it, I believe, even as a very old man. His broad forehead, built for thinking, was the seat of an imperturbable cheerfulness and joy. Speech, the richest in thought, flowed from his lips. Playfulness, wit, and humor were at his command. His lectures were the most entertaining talks. His mind, which examined Leibniz, Wolff, Baumgarten, Crusius, and Hume, and investigated the laws of nature of Newton, Kepler, and the physicists, comprehended equally the newest works of Rousseau . . . and the latest discoveries in science. He weighed them all, and always came back to the unbiased knowledge of nature and to the moral worth of man. The history of men and peoples, natural history and science, mathematics and observation, were the sources from which he enlivened his lectures and conversation. He was indifferent to nothing worth knowing. No cabal, no sect, no prejudice, no desire for fame could ever tempt him in the slightest away from broadening and illuminating the truth. He incited and gently forced others to think for themselves; despotism was foreign to his mind. This man, whom I name with the greatest gratitude and respect, was Immanuel Kant.

L.W. B.

# SELECTED BIBLIOGRAPHY

## I. GERMAN EDITIONS

*Kants Gesammelte Schriften*

Published by the Preussische Akademie der Wissenschaften, 23 volumes, 1900-1956. *Grundlegung zur Metaphysik der Sitten,* edited by Paul Menzer, in Volume IV (1911).

*Kants Werke*

Edited by Ernst Cassirer; published Berlin: Bruno Cassirer, 1912-22. 11 volumes. *Grundlegung,* edited by Ernst Cassirer and Arthur Buchenau, in Volume IV.

*Grundlegung zur Metaphysik der Sitten*

Edited by Karl Vorländer. In the series "Philosophische Bibliothek," Leipzig and Hamburg: Felix Meiner, 1906; third edition, reprint, 1952.

## II. STUDIES OF THE *FOUNDATIONS*

Beck, Lewis White. *A Commentary on Kant's Critique of Practical Reason.* Chicago, 1960.

Duncan, A. R. C. *Practical Reason and Morality. A Study of Immanuel Kant's Foundations for the Metaphysics of Morals.* Edinburgh [1957].

Paton, H. J. *The Categorical Imperative. A Study in Kant's Moral Philosophy.* London: Hutchinson [1946]; Chicago, 1948.

Ross, Sir William David. *Kant's Ethical Theory. A Commentary on the* Grundlegung zur Metaphysik der Sitten. Oxford, 1954.

Scott, John Waugh. *Kant on the Moral Life: An Exposition of Kant's "Grundlegung."* London, 1924.

# NOTE ON THE TEXT

This volume contains slightly revised versions of my translation of *Foundations of the Metaphysics of Morals* and of *What Is Enlightenment?* as published in the volume *Kant's Critique of Practical Reason and other Writings in Moral Philosophy* (Chicago: University of Chicago Press, 1949). They were reprinted with a new introduction by the University of Chicago Press in 1950; the Introduction to the present volume is slightly revised from that first published in 1950. The page numbers inserted in the text and running heads are those of the Akademie edition.

L. W. B.

# FOUNDATIONS OF THE
# METAPHYSICS OF MORALS

# I

# FOUNDATIONS OF THE METAPHYSICS
# OF MORALS

## PREFACE

Ancient Greek philosophy was divided into three [387] sciences: physics, ethics, and logic. This division conforms perfectly to the nature of the subject, and one can improve on it perhaps only by supplying its principle in order both to insure its exhaustiveness and to define correctly the necessary subdivisions.

All rational knowledge is either material, and concerns some object, or formal, and is occupied merely with the form of understanding and reason itself and with the universal rules of thinking without regard to distinctions between objects. Formal philosophy is called logic. Material philosophy, however, which has to do with definite objects and the laws to which they are subject, is itself divided into two parts. This is because these laws are either laws of nature or laws of freedom. The science of the former is called physics and that of the latter ethics. The former is also called theory of nature and the latter theory of morals.

Logic can have no empirical part—a part in which universal and necessary laws of thinking would rest upon grounds taken from experience. For in that case it would not be logic, i.e., a canon for understanding or reason which is valid for all thinking and which must be demonstrated. But, on the other hand, natural and moral philosophy can each have its empirical part. The former must do so, for it must determine the laws of nature as an object of experience, and the latter because it must determine the human will so far as it is affected by nature. The laws of the former are laws according to [388] which everything happens; those of the latter are laws according to which everything should happen, but allow for conditions under which what should happen often does not.

All philosophy, so far as it is based on experience, may be called empirical; but, so far as it presents its doctrines solely on the basis of a priori principles, it may be called pure philosophy. The latter, when merely formal, is logic; when limited to definite objects of understanding, it is metaphysics.

In this way there arises the idea of a twofold metaphysics— a metaphysics of nature and a metaphysics of morals. Physics, therefore, will have an empirical and also a rational part, and ethics likewise. In ethics, however, the empirical part may be called more specifically practical anthropology; the rational part, morals proper.

All crafts, handiworks, and arts have gained by the division of labor, for when one person does not do everything, but each limits himself to a particular job which is distinguished from all the others by the treatment it requires, he can do it with greater perfection and with more facility. Where work is not thus differentiated and divided, where everyone is a jack-of-all-trades, the crafts remain at a barbaric level. It might be worth considering whether pure philosophy in each of its parts does not require a man particularly devoted to it, and whether it would not be better for the learned profession as a whole to warn those who are in the habit of catering to the taste of the public by mixing up the empirical with the rational in all sorts of proportions which they do not themselves know and who call themselves independent thinkers (giving the name of speculator to those who apply themselves to the merely rational part). This warning would be that they should not at one and the same time carry on two employments which differ widely in the treatment they require, and for each of which perhaps a special talent is needed since the combination of these talents in one person produces only bunglers. I ask only whether the nature of the science does not require that a careful separation of the empirical from the rational part be made, with a metaphysics of nature put before real (empirical)

physics and a metaphysics of morals before practical anthropology. These prior sciences [1] must be carefully purified of
everything empirical so that we can know how much pure
reason can accomplish in each case and from what sources [389]
it creates its a priori teaching, whether the latter inquiry be
conducted by all moralists (whose name is legion) or only by
some who feel a calling to it.

Since my purpose here is directed to moral philosophy, I
narrow the proposed question to this: Is it not of the utmost
necessity to construct a pure moral philosophy which is completely freed from everything which may be only empirical
and thus belong to anthropology? That there must be such a
philosophy is self-evident from the common idea of duty and
moral laws. Everyone must admit that a law, if it is to hold
morally, i.e., as a ground of obligation, must imply absolute
necessity; he must admit that the command, "Thou shalt not
lie," does not apply to men only, as if other rational beings
had no need to observe it. The same is true for all other moral
laws properly so called. He must concede that the ground of
obligation here must not be sought in the nature of man or
in the circumstances in which he is placed, but sought a priori
solely in the concepts of pure reason, and that every other
precept which rests on principles of mere experience, even
a precept which is in certain respects universal, so far as it
leans in the least on empirical grounds (perhaps only in regard
to the motive involved), may be called a practical rule but
never a moral law.

Thus not only are moral laws together with their principles
essentially different from all practical knowledge in which
there is anything empirical, but all moral philosophy rests
solely on its pure part. Applied to man, it borrows nothing
from knowledge of him (anthropology) but gives him, as a
rational being, a priori laws. No doubt these laws require a
power of judgment sharpened by experience, partly in order
to decide in what cases they apply and partly to procure for
them an access to man's will and an impetus to their practice.

1 [Reading the plural with the Academy ed.]

For man is affected by so many inclinations that, though he is capable of the idea of a practical pure reason, he is not so easily able to make it concretely effective in the conduct of his life.

A metaphysics of morals is therefore indispensable, not merely because of motives to speculate on the source of [390] the a priori practical principles which lie in our reason, but also because morals themselves remain subject to all kinds of corruption so long as the guide and supreme norm for their correct estimation is lacking. For it is not sufficient to that which should be morally good that it conform to the law; it must be done for the sake of the law. Otherwise the conformity is merely contingent and spurious, because, though the unmoral ground may indeed now and then produce lawful actions, more often it brings forth unlawful ones. But the moral law can be found in its purity and genuineness (which is the central concern in the practical) nowhere else than in a pure philosophy; therefore, this (i.e., metaphysics) must lead the way, and without it there can be no moral philosophy. Philosophy which mixes pure principles with empirical ones does not deserve the name, for what distinguishes philosophy from common rational knowledge is its treatment in separate sciences of what is confusedly comprehended in such knowledge. Much less does it deserve the name of moral philosophy, since by this confusion it spoils the purity of morals themselves and works contrary to its own end.

It should not be thought that what is here required is already present in the celebrated Wolff's propaedeutic to his moral philosophy, i.e., in what he calls universal practical philosophy, and that it is not an entirely new field that is to be opened. Precisely because his work was to be universal practical philosophy, it deduced no will of any particular kind, such as one determined without any empirical motives but completely by a priori principles; in a word, it had nothing which could be called a pure will, since it considered only volition in general with all the actions and conditions which pertain to it in this general sense. Thus his propaedeutic differs from a metaphysics of morals in the same way that general logic is distinguished from transcendental philosophy, the former expounding the actions and rules of thinking in general, and the latter presenting the particular actions and rules of pure thinking, i.e., of thinking by which objects are known completely a priori. For the metaphysics of morals is meant to investigate the idea and principles of a possible pure will and not the actions and conditions of the human volition as such, which are for the most part drawn from psychology.

That in general practical philosophy laws and duty are [391] discussed (though improperly) is no objection to my assertion. For the authors of this science remain even here true to their idea of it. They do not distinguish the motives which are presented completely a priori by reason alone, and which are thus moral in the proper sense of the word, from the empirical motives which the understanding, by comparing experiences, elevates to universal concepts. Rather, they consider motives without regard to the difference in their source but only with reference to their greater or smaller number (as they are considered to be all of the same kind); they thus formulate their concept of obligation, which is anything but moral, but which is all that can be desired in a philosophy that does not decide whether the origin of all possible practical concepts is a priori or only a posteriori.

As a preliminary to a metaphysics of morals which I intend some day to publish, I issue these *Foundations*. There is, to be sure, no other foundation for such a metaphysics than a critical examination of a pure practical reason, just as there is no other foundation for metaphysics than the already published critical examination of the pure speculative reason. But, in the first place, a critical examination of pure practical reason is not of such extreme importance as that of speculative reason, because human reason, even in the commonest mind, can easily be brought to a high degree of correctness and completeness in moral matters, while, on the other hand, in its theoretical but pure use it is entirely dialectical. In the second place, I require of a critical examination of a pure practical reason, if it is to be complete, that its unity with the speculative be subject to presentation under a common principle, because in the final analysis there can be but one and the same reason which must be differentiated only in application. But I could not bring this to such a completeness without bringing in observations of an altogether different kind and without thereby confusing the reader. For these reasons I have employed the title, *Foundations of the Metaphysics of Morals,* instead of *Critique of Pure Practical Reason.*

Because, in the third place, a metaphysics of morals, in spite of its forbidding title, is capable of a high degree of popularity and adaptation to common understanding, I find it useful to separate this preliminary work of laying the foundation in order not to have to introduce unavoid- [392] able subtleties into the later, more comprehensive, work.

The present foundations, however, are nothing more than the search for and establishment of the supreme principle of morality. This constitutes a task altogether complete in its intention and one which should be kept separate from all other moral inquiry.

My conclusions concerning this important question, which has not yet been discussed nearly enough, would, of course, be clarified by application of the principle to the whole system of morality, and it would receive much confirmation by the adequacy which it would everywhere show. But I must forego this advantage, which would in the final analysis be more privately gratifying than commonly useful, because ease of use and apparent adequacy of a principle are not any sure proof of its correctness, but rather awaken a certain partiality which prevents a rigorous investigation and evaluation of it for itself without regard to consequences.

I have adopted in this writing the method which is, I think, most suitable if one wishes to proceed analytically from common knowledge to the determination of its supreme principle, and then synthetically from the examination of this principle and its sources back to common knowledge where it finds its application. The division is therefore as follows:

1. First Section. Transition from the Common Rational Knowledge of Morals to the Philosophical
2. Second Section. Transition from the Popular Moral Philosophy to the Metaphysics of Morals
3. Third Section. Final Step from the Metaphysics of Morals to the Critical Examination of Pure Practical Reason.

## FIRST SECTION

## TRANSITION FROM THE COMMON RATIONAL KNOWLEDGE OF MORALS TO THE PHILOSOPHICAL

Nothing in the world—indeed nothing even beyond [393] the world—can possibly be conceived which could be called good without qualification except a *good will*. Intelligence, wit, judgment, and the other talents of the mind, however they may be named, or courage, resoluteness, and perseverance as qualities of temperament, are doubtless in many respects good and desirable. But they can become extremely bad and harmful if the will, which is to make use of these gifts of nature and which in its special constitution is called character, is not good. It is the same with the gifts of fortune. Power, riches, honor, even health, general well-being, and the contentment with one's condition which is called happiness, make for pride and even arrogance if there is not a good will to correct their influence on the mind and on its principles of action so as to make it universally conformable to its end. It need hardly be mentioned that the sight of a being adorned with no feature of a pure and good will, yet enjoying uninterrupted prosperity, can never give pleasure to a rational impartial observer. Thus the good will seems to constitute the indispensable condition even of worthiness to be happy.

Some qualities seem to be conducive to this good will and can facilitate its action, but, in spite of that, they have [394] no intrinsic unconditional worth. They rather presuppose a good will, which limits the high esteem which one otherwise rightly has for them and prevents their being held to be absolutely good. Moderation in emotions and passions, self-control, and calm deliberation not only are good in many respects but even seem to constitute a part of the inner worth of the person. But however unconditionally they were esteemed by the ancients, they are far from being good without qualification. For without the principle of a good will they can become extremely bad, and the coolness of a villain makes him not only far more dangerous but also more directly abominable in our eyes than he would have seemed without it.

The good will is not good because of what it effects or accomplishes or because of its adequacy to achieve some proposed end; it is good only because of its willing, i.e., it is good of itself. And, regarded for itself, it is to be esteemed incomparably higher than anything which could be brought about by it in favor of any inclination or even of the sum total of all inclinations. Even if it should happen that, by a particularly unfortunate fate or by the niggardly provision of a stepmotherly nature, this will should be wholly lacking in power to accomplish its purpose, and if even the greatest effort should not avail it to achieve anything of its end, and if there remained only the good will (not as a mere wish but as the summoning of all the means in our power), it would sparkle like a jewel in its own right, as something that had its full worth in itself. Usefulness or fruitlessness can neither diminish nor augment this worth. Its usefulness would be only its setting, as it were, so as to enable us to handle it more conveniently in commerce or to attract the attention of those who are not yet connoisseurs, but not to recommend it to those who are experts or to determine its worth.

But there is something so strange in this idea of the absolute worth of the will alone, in which no account is taken of any use, that, notwithstanding the agreement even of common sense, the suspicion must arise that perhaps only high-flown fancy is its hidden basis, and that we may have misunder- [395] stood the purpose of nature in its appointment of reason as the ruler of our will. We shall therefore examine this idea from this point of view.

In the natural constitution of an organized being, i.e., one suitably adapted to life, we assume as an axiom that no organ will be found for any purpose which is not the fittest and best adapted to that purpose. Now if its preservation, its welfare—in a word, its happiness—were the real end of nature in a being having reason and will, then nature would have hit upon a very poor arrangement in appointing the reason of the creature to be the executor of this purpose. For all the actions which the creature has to perform with this intention, and the entire rule of its conduct, would be dictated much more exactly by instinct, and that end would be far more certainly attained by instinct than it ever could be by reason. And if, over and above this, reason should have been granted to the favored creature, it would have served only to let it contemplate the happy constitution of its nature, to admire it, to rejoice in it, and to be grateful for it to its beneficent cause. But reason would not have been given in order that the being should subject its faculty of desire to that weak and delusive guidance and to meddle with the purpose of nature. In a word, nature would have taken care that reason did not break forth into practical use nor have the presumption, with its weak insight, to think out for itself the plan of happiness and the means of attaining it. Nature would have taken over not only the choice of ends but also that of the means, and with wise foresight she would have entrusted both to instinct alone.

And, in fact, we find that the more a cultivated reason deliberately devotes itself to the enjoyment of life and happiness, the more the man falls short of true contentment. From this fact there arises in many persons, if only they are candid enough to admit it, a certain degree of misology, hatred of reason. This is particularly the case with those who are most experienced in its use. After counting all the advantages which they draw—I will not say from the invention of the arts of common luxury—from the sciences (which in the end seem to them to be also a luxury of the understanding), they nevertheless find that they have actually brought more trouble on their shoulders instead of gaining in happiness; they [396] finally envy, rather than despise, the common run of men who are better guided by mere natural instinct and who do not permit their reason much influence on their conduct. And we must at least admit that a morose attitude or ingratitude to the goodness with which the world is governed is by no means found always among those who temper or refute the boasting eulogies which are given of the advantages of happiness and contentment with which reason is supposed to supply us. Rather their judgment is based on the idea of another and far more worthy purpose of their existence for which, instead of happiness, their reason is properly intended, this purpose, therefore, being the supreme condition to which the private purposes of men must for the most part defer.

Reason is not, however, competent to guide the will safely with regard to its objects and the satisfaction of all our needs (which it in part multiplies), and to this end an innate instinct would have led with far more certainty. But reason is given to us as a practical faculty, i.e., one which is meant to have an influence on the will. As nature has elsewhere distributed capacities suitable to the functions they are to perform, reason's proper function must be to produce a will good in itself and not one good merely as a means, for to the former reason is absolutely essential. This will must indeed not be the sole and complete good but the highest good and the condition of all others, even of the desire for happiness. In this case it is entirely compatible with the wisdom of nature that the cultivation of reason, which is required for the former unconditional purpose, at least in this life restricts in many ways—indeed can reduce to less than nothing—the achievement of the latter conditional purpose, happiness. For one perceives that nature here does not proceed unsuitably to its purpose, because reason, which recognizes its highest practical vocation in the establishment of a good will, is capable only of a contentment of its own kind, i.e., one that springs from the attainment of a purpose which is determined by reason, even though this injures the ends of inclination.

We have, then, to develop the concept of a will which [397] is to be esteemed as good of itself without regard to anything else. It dwells already in the natural sound understanding and does not need so much to be taught as only to be brought to light. In the estimation of the total worth of our actions it always takes first place and is the condition of everything else. In order to show this, we shall take the concept of duty. It contains that of a good will, though with certain subjective restrictions and hindrances; but these are far from concealing it and making it unrecognizable, for they rather bring it out by contrast and make it shine forth all the brighter.

I here omit all actions which are recognized as opposed to duty, even though they may be useful in one respect or another, for with these the question does not arise at all as to whether they may be carried out *from* duty, since they conflict with it. I also pass over the actions which are really in accordance with duty and to which one has no direct inclination, rather executing them because impelled to do so by another inclination. For it is easily decided whether an action in accord with duty is performed from duty or for some selfish purpose. It is far more difficult to note this difference when the action is in accordance with duty and, in addition, the subject has a direct inclination to do it. For example, it is in fact in accordance with duty that a dealer should not overcharge an inexperienced customer, and wherever there is much business the prudent merchant does not do so, having a fixed price for everyone, so that a child may buy of him as cheaply as any other. Thus the customer is honestly served. But this is far from sufficient to justify the belief that the merchant has behaved in this way from duty and principles of honesty. His own advantage required this behavior; but it cannot be assumed that over and above that he had a direct inclination to the purchaser and that, out of love, as it were, he gave none an advantage in price over another. Therefore the action was done neither from duty nor from direct inclination but only for a selfish purpose.

On the other hand, it is a duty to preserve one's life, and moreover everyone has a direct inclination to do so. But for that reason the often anxious care which most men take of it has no intrinsic worth, and the maxim of doing so has no [398] moral import. They preserve their lives according to duty, but not from duty. But if adversities and hopeless sorrow completely take away the relish for life, if an unfortunate man, strong in soul, is indignant rather than despondent or dejected over his fate and wishes for death, and yet preserves his life without loving it and from neither inclination nor fear but from duty—then his maxim has a moral import.

To be kind where one can is duty, and there are, moreover, many persons so sympathetically constituted that without any motive of vanity or selfishness they find an inner satisfaction in spreading joy, and rejoice in the contentment of others which they have made possible. But I say that, however dutiful and amiable it may be, that kind of action has no true moral worth. It is on a level with [actions arising from] other inclinations, such as the inclination to honor, which, if fortunately directed to what in fact accords with duty and is generally useful and thus honorable, deserve praise and encouragement but no esteem. For the maxim lacks the moral import of an action done not from inclination but from duty. But assume that the mind of that friend to mankind was clouded by a sorrow of his own which extinguished all sympathy with the lot of others and that he still had the power to benefit others in distress, but that their need left him untouched because he was preoccupied with his own need. And now suppose him to tear himself, unsolicited by inclination, out of this dead insensibility and to perform this action only from duty and without any inclination—then for the first time his action has genuine moral worth. Furthermore, if nature has put little sympathy in the heart of a man, and if he, though an honest man, is by temperament cold and indifferent to the sufferings of others, perhaps because he is provided with special gifts of patience and fortitude and expects or even requires that others should have the same—and such a man would certainly not be the meanest product of nature—would not he find in himself a source from which to give himself a far higher worth than he could have got by having a good-natured temperament? This is unquestionably true even though nature did not make him philanthropic, for it is just here that the worth of the character is brought out, which is morally and incomparably the highest of all: he is benef- [399] icent not from inclination but from duty.

To secure one's own happiness is at least indirectly a duty, for discontent with one's condition under pressure from many cares and amid unsatisfied wants could easily become a great temptation to transgress duties. But without any view to duty all men have the strongest and deepest inclination to happiness, because in this idea all inclinations are summed up. But the precept of happiness is often so formulated that it definitely thwarts some inclinations, and men can make no definite and certain concept of the sum of satisfaction of all inclinations which goes under the name of happiness. It is not to be wondered at, therefore, that a single inclination, definite as to what it promises and as to the time at which it can be satisfied, can outweigh a fluctuating idea, and that, for example, a man with the gout can choose to enjoy what he likes and to suffer what he may, because according to his calculations at least on this occasion he has not sacrificed the enjoyment of the present moment to a perhaps groundless expectation of a happiness supposed to lie in health. But even in this case, if the universal inclination to happiness did not determine his will, and if health were not at least for him a necessary factor in these calculations, there yet would remain, as in all other cases, a law that he ought to promote his happiness, not from inclination but from duty. Only from this law would his conduct have true moral worth.

It is in this way, undoubtedly, that we should understand those passages of Scripture which command us to love our neighbor and even our enemy, for love as an inclination cannot be commanded. But beneficence from duty, when no inclination impels it and even when it is opposed by a natural and unconquerable aversion, is practical love, not pathological love; it resides in the will and not in the propensities of feeling, in principles of action and not in tender sympathy; and it alone can be commanded.

[Thus the first proposition of morality is that to have moral worth an action must be done from duty.] The second proposition is: An action performed from duty does not have its moral worth in the purpose which is to be achieved through it but in the maxim by which it is determined. Its moral value, therefore, does not depend on the realization of the object of the action but merely on the principle of volition by [400] which the action is done, without any regard to the objects of the faculty of desire. From the preceding discussion it is clear that the purposes we may have for our actions and their effects as ends and incentives of the will cannot give the actions any unconditional and moral worth. Wherein, then, can this worth lie, if it is not in the will in relation to its hoped-for effect? It can lie nowhere else than in the principle of the will, irrespective of the ends which can be realized by such action. For the will stands, as it were, at the crossroads halfway between its a priori principle which is formal and its a posteriori incentive which is material. Since it must be determined by something, if it is done from duty it must be determined by the formal principle of volition as such since every material principle has been withdrawn from it.

The third principle, as a consequence of the two preceding, I would express as follows: Duty is the necessity of an action executed from respect for law. I can certainly have an inclination to the object as an effect of the proposed action, but I can never have respect for it precisely because it is a mere effect and not an activity of a will. Similarly, I can have no respect for any inclination whatsoever, whether my own or that of another; in the former case I can at most approve of it and in the latter I can even love it, i.e., see it as favorable to my own advantage. But that which is connected with my will merely as ground and not as consequence, that which does not serve my inclination but overpowers it or at least excludes it from being considered in making a choice—in a word, law itself—can be an object of respect and thus a command. Now as an act from duty wholly excludes the influence of inclination and therewith every object of the will, nothing remains which can determine the will objectively except the law, and nothing subjectively except pure respect for this practical law. This subjective element is the maxim [1] that I ought to follow such a law even if it thwarts all my inclinations.    [401]

Thus the moral worth of an action does not lie in the effect which is expected from it or in any principle of action which has to borrow its motive from this expected effect. For all these effects (agreeableness of my own condition, indeed even the promotion of the happiness of others) could be brought about through other causes and would not require the will of a rational being, while the highest and unconditional good can be found only in such a will. Therefore, the pre-eminent good can consist only in the conception of the law in itself (which can be present only in a rational being) so far as this conception and not the hoped-for effect is the determining ground of the will. This pre-eminent good, which we call moral, is already present in the person who acts according to this conception, and we do not have to look for it first in the result.[2]

---

[1] A maxim is the subjective principle of volition. The objective principle (i.e., that which would serve all rational beings also subjectively as a practical principle if reason had full power over the faculty of desire) is the practical law.

[2] It might be objected that I seek to take refuge in an obscure feeling behind the word "respect," instead of clearly resolving the question with a concept of reason. But though respect is a feeling, it is not one received through any [outer] influence but is self-wrought by a rational concept; thus it differs specifically from all feelings of the former kind which may be referred to inclination or fear. What I recognize directly as a law for myself I recognize with respect, which means merely the consciousness of the submission of my will to a law without the intervention of other influences on my mind. The direct determination of the will by the law and

But what kind of a law can that be, the conception of [402] which must determine the will without reference to the expected result? Under this condition alone the will can be called absolutely good without qualification. Since I have robbed the will of all impulses which could come to it from obedience to any law, nothing remains to serve as a principle of the will except universal conformity of its action to law as such. That is, I should never act in such a way that I could not also will that my maxim should be a universal law. Mere conformity to law as such (without assuming any particular law applicable to certain actions) serves as the principle of the will, and it must serve as such a principle if duty is not to be a vain delusion and chimerical concept. The common reason of mankind in its practical judgments is in perfect agreement with this and has this principle constantly in view.

Let the question, for example, be: May I, when in distress, make a promise with the intention not to keep it? I easily distinguish the two meanings which the question can have, viz., whether it is prudent to make a false promise, or whether it conforms to my duty. Undoubtedly the former can often be the case, though I do see clearly that it is not sufficient merely to escape from the present difficulty by this expedient, but that I must consider whether inconveniences much greater than the present one may not later spring from this lie. Even with all

---

the consciousness of this determination is respect; thus respect can be regarded as the effect of the law on the subject and not as the cause of the law. Respect is properly the conception of a worth which thwarts my self-love. Thus it is regarded as an object neither of inclination nor of fear, though it has something analogous to both. The only object of respect is the law, and indeed only the law which we impose on ourselves and yet recognize as necessary in itself. As a law, we are subject to it without consulting self-love; as imposed on us by ourselves, it is a consequence of our will. In the former respect it is analogous to fear and in the latter to inclination. All respect for a person is only respect for the law (of righteousness, etc.) of which the person provides an example. Because we see the improvement of our talents as a duty, we think of a person of talents as the example of a law, as it were (the law that we should by practice become like him in his talents), and that constitutes our respect. All so-called moral interest consists solely in respect for the law.

my supposed cunning, the consequences cannot be so easily foreseen. Loss of credit might be far more disadvantageous than the misfortune I now seek to avoid, and it is hard to tell whether it might not be more prudent to act according to a universal maxim and to make it a habit not to promise anything without intending to fulfill it. But it is soon clear to me that such a maxim is based only on an apprehensive concern with consequences.

To be truthful from duty, however, is an entirely different thing from being truthful out of fear of disadvantageous consequences, for in the former case the concept of the action itself contains a law for me, while in the latter I must first look about to see what results for me may be connected with it. For to deviate from the principle of duty is certainly bad, but to be unfaithful to my maxim of prudence can sometimes be very [403] advantageous to me, though it is certainly safer to abide by it. The shortest but most infallible way to find the answer to the question as to whether a deceitful promise is consistent with duty is to ask myself: Would I be content that my maxim (of extricating myself from difficulty by a false promise) should hold as a universal law for myself as well as for others? And could I say to myself that everyone may make a false promise when he is in a difficulty from which he otherwise cannot escape? I immediately see that I could will the lie but not a universal law to lie. For with such a law there would be no promises at all, inasmuch as it would be futile to make a pretense of my intention in regard to future actions to those who would not believe this pretense or—if they overhastily did so—who would pay me back in my own coin. Thus my maxim would necessarily destroy itself as soon as it was made a universal law.

I do not, therefore, need any penetrating acuteness in order to discern what I have to do in order that my volition may be morally good. Inexperienced in the course of the world, incapable of being prepared for all its contingencies, I ask myself only: Can I will that my maxim become a universal law? If not, it must be rejected, not because of any disadvantage accruing to myself or even to others, but because it cannot enter as a principle into a possible universal legislation, and reason extorts from me an immediate respect for such legislation. I do not as yet discern on what it is grounded (a question the philosopher may investigate), but I at least understand that it is an estimation of the worth which far outweighs all the worth of whatever is recommended by the inclinations, and that the necessity of my actions from pure respect for the practical law constitutes duty. To duty every other motive must give place, because duty is the condition of a will good in itself, whose worth transcends everything.

Thus within the moral knowledge of common human reason we have attained its principle. To be sure, common human reason does not think of it abstractly in such a universal form, but it always has it in view and uses it as the standard of [404] its judgments. It would be easy to show how common human reason, with this compass, knows well how to distinguish what is good, what is bad, and what is consistent or inconsistent with duty. Without in the least teaching common reason anything new, we need only to draw its attention to its own principle, in the manner of Socrates, thus showing that neither science nor philosophy is needed in order to know what one has to do in order to be honest and good, and even wise and virtuous. We might have conjectured beforehand that the knowledge of what everyone is obliged to do and thus also to know would be within the reach of everyone, even the most ordinary man. Here we cannot but admire the great advantages which the practical faculty of judgment has over the theoretical in ordinary human understanding. In the theoretical, if ordinary reason ventures to go beyond the laws of experience and perceptions of the senses, it falls into sheer inconceivabilities and self-contradictions, or at least into a chaos of uncertainty, obscurity, and instability. In the practical, on the other hand, the power of judgment first shows itself to advantage when common understanding excludes all sensuous incentives from practical laws. It then becomes even subtle, quibbling with its own conscience or with other claims to what should be called right, or wishing to determine correctly for its own instruction the worth of certain actions. But the most remarkable thing about ordinary reason in its practical concern is that it may have as much hope as any philosopher of hitting the mark. In fact, it is almost more certain to do so than the philosopher, because he has no principle which the common understanding lacks, while his judgment is easily confused by a mass of irrelevant considerations, so that it easily turns aside from the correct way. Would it not, therefore, be wiser in moral matters to acquiesce in the common rational judgment, or at most to call in philosophy in order to make the system of morals more complete and comprehensible and its rules more convenient for use (especially in disputation) than to steer the common understanding from its happy simplicity in practical matters and to lead it through philosophy into a new path of inquiry and instruction?

Innocence is indeed a glorious thing, but, on the other [405] hand, it is very sad that it cannot well maintain itself, being easily led astray. For this reason, even wisdom—which consists more in acting than in knowing—needs science, not to learn from it but to secure admission and permanence to its precepts. Man feels in himself a powerful counterpoise against all commands of duty which reason presents to him as so deserving of respect; this counterpoise is his needs and inclinations, the complete satisfaction of which he sums up under the name of happiness. Now reason issues inexorable commands without promising anything to the inclinations. It disregards, as it were, and holds in contempt those claims which are so impetuous and yet so plausible, and which will not allow themselves to be abolished by any command. From this a natural dialectic arises, i.e., a propensity to argue against the stern laws of duty and their validity, or at least to place their purity and strictness in doubt and, where possible, to make them more accordant with our wishes and inclinations. This is equivalent to corrupting them in their very foundations and destroying their dignity—a thing which even common practical reason cannot ultimately call good.

In this way common human reason is impelled to go outside its sphere and to take a step into the field of practical philosophy. But it is forced to do so not by any speculative need, which never occurs to it so long as it is satisfied to remain merely healthy reason; rather, it is so impelled on practical grounds in order to obtain information and clear instruction respecting the source of its principle and the correct determination of this principle in its opposition to the maxims which are based on need and inclination. It seeks this information in order to escape from the perplexity of opposing claims and to avoid the danger of losing all genuine moral principles through the equivocation in which it is easily involved. Thus, when practical common reason cultivates itself, a dialectic surreptitiously ensues which forces it to seek aid in philosophy, just as the same thing happens in the theoretical use of reason. In this case, as in the theoretical, it will find rest only in a thorough critical examination of our reason.

## SECOND SECTION

## TRANSITION FROM THE POPULAR MORAL PHILOSOPHY TO THE METAPHYSICS OF MORALS

If we have derived our earlier concept of duty from [406] the common use of our practical reason, it is by no means to be inferred that we have treated it as an empirical concept. On the contrary, if we attend to our experience of the way men act, we meet frequent and, as we ourselves confess, justified complaints that we cannot cite a single sure example of the disposition to act from pure duty. There are also justified complaints that, though much may be done that accords with what duty commands, it is nevertheless always doubtful whether it is done from duty, and thus whether it has moral worth. There have always been philosophers who for this reason have absolutely denied the reality of this disposition in human actions, attributing everything to more or less refined self-love. They have done so without questioning the correctness of the concept of morality. Rather they have spoken with sincere regret of the frailty and corruption of human nature, which is noble enough to take as its precept an idea so worthy of respect but which at the same time is too weak to follow it, employing reason, which should legislate for human nature, only to provide for the interest of the inclinations either singly or, at best, in their greatest possible harmony with one another.

It is in fact absolutely impossible by experience to dis- [407] cern with complete certainty a single case in which the maxim of an action, however much it may conform to duty, rested solely on moral grounds and on the conception of one's duty. It sometimes happens that in the most searching self-examination we can find nothing except the moral ground of duty which could have been powerful enough to move us to this or that good action and to such great sacrifice. But from this we cannot by any means conclude with certainty that a secret impulse of self-love, falsely appearing as the idea of duty, was not actually the true determining cause of the will. For we like to flatter ourselves with a pretended nobler motive, while in fact even the strictest examination can never lead us entirely behind the secret incentives, for, when moral worth is in question, it is not a matter of actions which one sees but of their inner principles which one does not see.

Moreover, one cannot better serve the wishes of those who ridicule all morality as a mere phantom of human imagination overreaching itself through self-conceit than by conceding to them that the concepts of duty must be derived only from experience (for they are ready to believe from indolence that this is true of all other concepts too). For, by this concession, a sure triumph is prepared for them. Out of love for humanity I am willing to admit that most of our actions are in accordance with duty; but, if we look more closely at our thoughts and aspirations, we everywhere come upon the dear self, which is always there, and it is this instead of the stern command of duty (which would often require self-denial) which supports our plans. One need not be an enemy of virtue, but only a cool observer who does not confuse even the liveliest aspiration for the good with its reality, to be doubtful sometimes whether true virtue can really be found anywhere in the world. This is especially true as one's years increase and one's power of judgment is made wiser by experience and more acute in observation. This being so, nothing can secure us against the complete abandonment of our ideas of duty and preserve in us a well-founded respect for its law except the clear conviction that, even if there never were actions springing [408] from such pure sources, our concern is not whether this or that was done but that reason of itself and independently of all appearances commands what ought to be done. Our concern is with actions of which perhaps the world has never had an example, with actions whose feasibility might be seriously doubted by those who base everything on experience, and yet with actions inexorably commanded by reason. For example, pure sincerity in friendship can be demanded of every man, and this demand is not in the least diminished if a sincere friend has never existed, because this duty, as duty in general, prior to all experience, lies in the idea of a reason which determines the will by a priori grounds.

It is clear that no experience can give occasion for inferring the possibility of such apodictic laws. This is especially clear when we add that, unless we wish to deny all truth to the concept of morality and renounce its application to any possible object, we cannot refuse to admit that the law of this concept is of such broad significance that it holds not merely for men but for all rational beings as such; we must grant that it must be valid with absolute necessity and not merely under contingent conditions and with exceptions. For with what right could we bring into unlimited respect something that might be valid only under contingent human conditions? And how could laws of the determination of our will be held to be laws of the determination of the will of a rational being in general and of ourselves in so far as we are rational beings, if they were merely empirical and did not have their origin completely a priori in pure, but practical, reason?

Nor could one give poorer counsel to morality than to attempt to derive it from examples. For each example of morality which is exhibited to me must itself have been previously judged according to principles of morality to see whether it is worthy to serve as an original example, i.e., as a model. By no means could it authoritatively furnish the concept of morality. Even the Holy One of the Gospel must be compared with our ideal of moral perfection before He is recognized as such; even He says of Himself, "Why call ye Me (whom you see) good? None is good (the archetype of the good) except God only (whom you do not see)." But whence do we have the concept of God as the highest good? Solely from the [409] idea of moral perfection which reason formulates a priori and which it inseparably connects with the concept of a free will. Imitation has no place in moral matters, and examples serve only for encouragement. That is, they put beyond question the practicability of what the law commands, and they make visible that which the practical rule expresses more generally. But they can never justify our guiding ourselves by examples and our setting aside their true original which lies in reason.

If there is thus no genuine supreme principle of morality which does not rest merely on pure reason independently of all experience, I do not believe it is necessary even to ask whether it is well to exhibit these concepts generally (*in abstracto*), which, together with the principles belonging to them, are established a priori. At any rate, this question need not be asked if knowledge which establishes this is to be distinguished from ordinary knowledge and called philosophical. But in our times this question may perhaps be necessary. For if we collected votes as to whether pure rational knowledge separated from all experience, i.e., metaphysics of morals, or popular practical philosophy is to be preferred, it is easily guessed on which side the majority would stand.

This condescension to popular notions is certainly very commendable once the ascent to the principles of pure reason has been satisfactorily accomplished. That would mean the prior establishment of the doctrine of morals on metaphysics and then, when it is established, to procure a hearing for it through popularization. But it is extremely absurd to want to achieve popularity in the first investigation, where everything depends on the correctness of the fundamental principles. Not only can this procedure never make claim to that rarest merit of true philosophical popularity, since there is really no art in being generally comprehensible if one thereby renounces all basic insight, but it produces a disgusting jumble of patched-up observations and half-reasoned principles. Shallowpates enjoy this, for it is very useful in everyday chitchat, while the more sensible feel confused and dissatisfied without being able to help themselves. They turn their eyes away, even though philosophers, who see very well through the delusion, find little audience when they call men away for a time [410] from this pretended popularization in order that they may rightly appear popular after they have attained a definite insight.

One need only look at the essays on morality which that popular taste favors. One will sometimes meet with the particular vocation of human nature (but occasionally also the idea of a rational nature in general), sometimes perfection, and sometimes happiness, here moral feeling, there fear of God, a little of this and a little of that in a marvelous mixture. However, it never occurs to the authors to ask whether the principles of morality are, after all, to be sought anywhere in knowledge of human nature (which we can derive only from experience). And if this is not the case, if the principles are completely a priori, free from everything empirical, and found exclusively in pure rational concepts and not at all in any other place, they never ask whether they should undertake this investigation as a separate inquiry, i.e., as pure practical philosophy or (if one may use a name so decried) a metaphysics [1] of morals. They never think of dealing with it alone

[1] If one wishes, the pure philosophy of morals (metaphysics) can be distinguished from the applied (i.e., applied to human nature), just as pure

and bringing it by itself to completeness, and of requiring the public, which desires popularization, to await the outcome of this undertaking.

But a completely isolated metaphysics of morals, mixed with no anthropology, no theology, no physics or hyperphysics, and even less with occult qualities (which might be called hypo-physical), is not only an indispensable substrate of all theo-retically sound and definite knowledge of duties; it is also a desideratum of the highest importance to the actual fulfill-ment of its precepts. For the pure conception of duty and of the moral law generally, with no admixture of empirical in-ducements, has an influence on the human heart so much more powerful than all other incentives [2] which may be [411] derived from the empirical field that reason, in the conscious-ness of its dignity, despises them and gradually becomes master over them. It has this influence only through reason, which thereby first realizes that it can of itself be practical. A mixed

---

mathematics and pure logic are distinguished from applied mathematics and applied logic. By this designation one is immediately reminded that moral principles are not founded on the peculiarities of human nature but must stand of themselves a priori, and that from such principles practical rules for every rational nature, and accordingly for man, must be derivable.

[2] I have a letter from the late excellent Sulzer * in which he asks me why the theories of virtue accomplish so little even though they contain so much that is convincing to reason. My answer was delayed in order that I might make it complete. The answer is only that the teachers themselves have not completely clarified their concepts, and when they wish to make up for this by hunting in every quarter for motives to the morally good so as to make their physic right strong, they spoil it. For the commonest observation shows that if we imagine an act of honesty performed with a steadfast soul and sundered from all view to any advantage in this or another world and even under the greatest temptations of need or allure-ment, it far surpasses and eclipses any similar action which was affected in the least by any foreign incentive; it elevates the soul and arouses the wish to be able to act in this way. Even moderately young children feel this impression, and one should never represent duties to them in any other way.

* [Johann Georg Sulzer (1720-79), an important figure at the court and in literary circles in Berlin. Cf. *Allgemeine deutsche Biographie*, XXXVII, 144-47.]

theory of morals which is put together both from incentives of feelings and inclinations and from rational concepts must, on the other hand, make the mind vacillate between motives which cannot be brought under any principle and which can lead only accidentally to the good and often to the bad.

From what has been said it is clear that all moral concepts have their seat and origin entirely a priori in reason. This is just as much the case in the most ordinary reason as in reason which is speculative to the highest degree. It is obvious that they cannot be abstracted from any empirical and hence merely contingent cognitions. In the purity of their origin lies their worthiness to serve us as supreme practical principles, and to the extent that something empirical is added to them just this much is subtracted from their genuine influence and from the unqualified worth of actions. Furthermore, it is evident that it is not only of the greatest necessity in a theoretical point of view when it is a question of speculation but also of the utmost practical importance to derive the concepts and laws of morals from pure reason and to present them pure and unmixed, and to determine the scope of this entire practical but pure rational knowledge (the entire faculty of pure practical reason) without making the principles depend upon [412] the particular nature of human reason as speculative philosophy may permit and even sometimes find necessary. But since moral laws should hold for every rational being as such, the principles must be derived from the universal concept of a rational being generally. In this manner all morals, which need anthropology for their application to men, must be completely developed first as pure philosophy, i.e., metaphysics, independently of anthropology (a thing which is easily done in such distinct fields of knowledge). For we know well that if we are not in possession of such a metaphysics, it is not merely futile to define accurately for the purposes of speculative judgment the moral element of duty in all actions which accord with duty, but impossible to base morals on legitimate principles for merely ordinary and practical use, especially in moral instruction; and it is only in this manner that pure moral dispositions can be produced and engrafted on men's minds for the purpose of the highest good in the world.

In this study we do not advance merely from the common moral judgment (which here is very worthy of respect) to the philosophical, as this has already been done, but we advance by natural stages from a popular philosophy (which goes no further than it can grope by means of examples) to metaphysics (which is not held back by anything empirical and which, as it must measure out the entire scope of rational knowledge of this kind, reaches even Ideas, where examples fail us). In order to make this advance, we must follow and clearly present the practical faculty of reason from its universal rules of determination to the point where the concept of duty arises from it.

Everything in nature works according to laws. Only a rational being has the capacity of acting according to the conception of laws, i.e., according to principles. This capacity is will. Since reason is required for the derivation of actions from laws, will is nothing else than practical reason. If reason infallibly determines the will, the actions which such a being recognizes as objectively necessary are also subjectively necessary. That is, the will is a faculty of choosing only that which reason, independently of inclination, recognizes as practically necessary, i.e., as good. But if reason of itself does not sufficiently determine the will, and if the will is subjugated to subjective conditions (certain incentives) which do not always agree with objective conditions; in a word, if the will is [413] not of itself in complete accord with reason (the actual case of men), then the actions which are recognized as objectively necessary are subjectively contingent, and the determination of such a will according to objective laws is constraint. That is, the relation of objective laws to a will which is not completely good is conceived as the determination of the will of a rational being by principles of reason to which this will is not by nature necessarily obedient.

The conception of an objective principle, so far as it con-
strains a will, is a command (of reason), and the formula of
this command is called an *imperative*.

All imperatives are expressed by an "ought" and thereby
indicate the relation of an objective law of reason to a will
which is not in its subjective constitution necessarily determined by this law. This relation is that of constraint. Imperatives say that it would be good to do or to refrain from doing
something, but they say it to a will which does not always do
something simply because it is presented as a good thing to do.
Practical good is what determines the will by means of the
conception of reason and hence not by subjective causes but,
rather, objectively, i.e., on grounds which are valid for every
rational being as such. It is distinguished from the pleasant
as that which has an influence on the will only by means of a
sensation from merely subjective causes, which hold only for
the senses of this or that person and not as a principle of
reason which holds for everyone.[3]

A perfectly good will, therefore, would be equally sub-  [414]
ject to objective laws (of the good), but it could not be conceived as constrained by them to act in accord with them,
because, according to its own subjective constitution, it can be

---

[3] The dependence of the faculty of desire on sensations is called [413]
inclination, and inclination always indicates a need. The dependence of a
contingently determinable will on principles of reason, however, is called
interest. An interest is present only in a dependent will which is not of
itself always in accord with reason; in the divine will we cannot conceive
of an interest. But even the human will can take an interest in something
without thereby acting from interest. The former means the practical interest in the action; the latter, the pathological interest in the object of
the action. The former indicates only the dependence of the will on
principles of reason in themselves, while the latter indicates dependence
on the principles of reason for the purpose of inclination, since reason
gives only the practical rule by which the needs of inclination are to be
aided.    In the former case the action interests me, and in the latter the
object of the action (so far as it is pleasant for me) interests me. In the
first section we have seen that, in the case of an action performed from
duty, no regard must be given to the interest in the object, but merely in
the action itself and its principle in reason (i.e., the law).

determined to act only through the conception of the good. Thus no imperatives hold for the divine will or, more generally, for a holy will. The "ought" is here out of place, for the volition of itself is necessarily in unison with the law. Therefore imperatives are only formulas expressing the relation of objective laws of volition in general to the subjective imperfection of the will of this or that rational being, e.g., the human will.

All imperatives command either hypothetically or categorically. The former present the practical necessity of a possible action as a means to achieving something else which one desires (or which one may possibly desire). The categorical imperative would be one which presented an action as of itself objectively necessary, without regard to any other end.

Since every practical law presents a possible action as good and thus as necessary for a subject practically determinable by reason, all imperatives are formulas of the determination of action which is necessary by the principle of a will which is in any way good. If the action is good only as a means to something else, the imperative is hypothetical; but if it is thought of as good in itself, and hence as necessary in a will which of itself conforms to reason as the principle of this will, the imperative is categorical.

The imperative thus says what action possible to me would be good, and it presents the practical rule in relation to a will which does not forthwith perform an action simply because it is good, in part because the subject does not always know that the action is good and in part (when he does know it) because his maxims can still be opposed to the objective principles of practical reason.

The hypothetical imperative, therefore, says only that the action is good to some purpose, possible or actual. In the [415] former case it is a problematical,[4] in the latter an assertorical,

---

4 [The *First Introduction to the Critique of Judgment* says: "This is the place to correct an error into which I fell in the *Foundations of the Metaphysics of Morals*. After I had stated that the imperatives of prudence commanded only conditionally, and indeed only under the condition of

practical principle. The categorical imperative, which declares the action to be of itself objectively necessary without making any reference to a purpose, i.e., without having any other end, holds as an apodictical (practical) principle.

We can think of that which is possible through the mere powers of some rational being as a possible purpose of any will. As a consequence, the principles of action, in so far as they are thought of as necessary to attain a possible purpose which can be achieved by them, are in reality infinitely numerous. All sciences have some practical part which consists of problems of some end which is possible for us and of imperatives as to how it can be reached. These can therefore generally be called imperatives of skill. Whether the end is reasonable and good is not in question at all, for the question is only of what must be done in order to attain it. The precepts to be followed by a physician in order to cure his patient and by a poisoner in order to bring about certain death are of equal value in so far as each does that which will perfectly accomplish his purpose. Since in early youth we do not know what ends may occur to us in the course of life, parents seek to let their children learn a great many things and provide for skill in the use of means to all sorts of arbitrary ends among which they cannot determine whether any one of them may later become an actual purpose of their pupil, though it is possible

---

merely possible, i.e., problematic, ends, I called that kind of practical precept 'problematic imperatives.' But there is certainly a contradiction in this expression. I should have called them 'technical imperatives,' i.e., imperatives of art. The pragmatic imperatives, or rules of prudence which command under the condition of an actual and even subjectively necessary end, belong also among the technical imperatives. (For what is prudence but the skill to use free men and even the natural dispositions and inclinations of oneself for one's own designs?) Only the fact that the end to which we submit ourselves and others, namely, our own happiness, does not belong to the merely arbitrary ends [which we may or may not have] justifies a special name for these imperatives because the problem does not require merely a mode of reaching the end as is the case with technical imperatives, but also requires a definition of what constitutes this end itself (happiness). The end must be presupposed as known in the case of technical imperatives" (Akademie ed., XX, 200 n.)]

that he may some day have it as his actual purpose. And this anxiety is so great that they commonly neglect to form and correct their judgment on the worth of things which they may make their ends.

There is one end, however, which we may presuppose as actual in all rational beings so far as imperatives apply to them, i.e., so far as they are dependent beings; there is one purpose not only which they *can* have but which we can presuppose that they all *do* have by a necessity of nature. This purpose is happiness. The hypothetical imperative which represents the practical necessity of action as means to the promotion of happiness is an assertorical imperative. We may not expound it as merely necessary to an uncertain and a merely possible purpose, but as necessary to a purpose which we can a priori and with assurance assume for everyone [416] because it belongs to his essence. Skill in the choice of means to one's own highest welfare can be called prudence [5] in the narrowest sense. Thus the imperative which refers to the choice of means to one's own happiness, i.e., the precept of prudence, is still only hypothetical; the action is not absolutely commanded but commanded only as a means to another end.

Finally, there is one imperative which directly commands a certain conduct without making its condition some purpose to be reached by it. This imperative is categorical. It concerns not the material of the action and its intended result but the form and the principle from which it results. What is essentially good in it consists in the intention, the result being what it may. This imperative may be called the imperative of morality.

Volition according to these three principles is plainly dis-

[5] The word "prudence" may be taken in two senses, and it may bear the name of prudence with reference to things of the world and private prudence. The former sense means the skill of a man in having an influence on others so as to use them for his own purposes. The latter is the ability to unite all these purposes to his own lasting advantage. The worth of the first is finally reduced to the latter, and of one who is prudent in the former sense but not in the latter we might better say that he is clever and cunning yet, on the whole, imprudent.

tinguished by dissimilarity in the constraint to which they subject the will. In order to clarify this dissimilarity, I believe that they are most suitably named if one says that they are either rules of skill, counsels of prudence, or commands (laws) of morality, respectively. For law alone implies the concept of an unconditional and objective and hence universally valid necessity, and commands are laws which must be obeyed, even against inclination. Counsels do indeed involve necessity, but a necessity that can hold only under a subjectively contingent condition, i.e., whether this or that man counts this or that as part of his happiness; but the categorical imperative, on the other hand, is restricted by no condition. As absolutely, though practically, necessary it can be called a command in the strict sense. We could also call the first imperative technical (belonging to art), the second pragmatic [6] (belonging to wel- [417] fare), and the third moral (belonging to free conduct as such, i.e., to morals).

The question now arises: how are all these imperatives possible? This question does not require an answer as to how the action which the imperative commands can be performed but merely as to how the constraint of the will, which the imperative expresses in the problem, can be conceived. How an imperative of skill is possible requires no particular discussion. Whoever wills the end, so far as reason has decisive influence on his action, wills also the indispensably necessary means to it that lie in his power. This proposition, in what concerns the will, is analytical; for, in willing an object as my effect, my causality as an acting cause, i.e., the use of the means, is already thought, and the imperative derives the concept of necessary actions to this end from the concept of willing this

---

[6] It seems to me that the proper meaning of the word "pragmatic" could be most accurately defined in this way. For sanctions which properly flow not from the law of states as necessary statutes but from provision for the general welfare are called pragmatic. A history is pragmatically composed when it teaches prudence, i.e., instructs the world how it could provide for its interest better than, or at least as well as, has been done in the past.

end. Synthetical propositions undoubtedly are necessary in determining the means to a proposed end, but they do not concern the ground, the act of the will, but only the way to make the object real. Mathematics teaches, by synthetical propositions only, that in order to bisect a line according to an infallible principle I must make two intersecting arcs from each of its extremities; but if I know the proposed result can be obtained only by such an action, then it is an analytical proposition that, if I fully will the effect, I must also will the action necessary to produce it. For it is one and the same thing to conceive of something as an effect which is in a certain way possible through me and to conceive of myself as acting in this way.

If it were only easy to give a definite concept of happiness, the imperatives of prudence would completely correspond to those of skill and would be likewise analytical. For it could be said in this case as well as in the former that whoever [418] wills the end wills also (necessarily according to reason) the only means to it which are in his power. But it is a misfortune that the concept of happiness is so indefinite that, although each person wishes to attain it, he can never definitely and self-consistently state what it is he really wishes and wills. The reason for this is that all elements which belong to the concept of happiness are empirical, i.e., they must be taken from experience, while for the idea of happiness an absolute whole, a maximum, of well-being is needed in my present and in every future condition. Now it is impossible even for a most clear-sighted and most capable but finite being to form here a definite concept of that which he really wills. If he wills riches, how much anxiety, envy, and intrigue might he not thereby draw upon his shoulders! If he wills much knowledge and vision, perhaps it might become only an eye that much sharper to show him as more dreadful the evils which are now hidden from him and which are yet unavoidable, or to burden his desires—which already sufficiently engage him—with even more needs! If he wills a long life, who guarantees that it will not be long misery? If he wills at least health, how often has not the discomfort of the body restrained him from excesses into which perfect health would have led him? In short, he is not capable, on any principle and with complete certainty, of ascertaining what would make him truly happy; omniscience would be needed for this. He cannot, therefore, act according to definite principles so as to be happy, but only according to empirical counsels, e.g., those of diet, economy, courtesy, restraint, etc., which are shown by experience best to promote welfare on the average. Hence the imperatives of prudence cannot, in the strict sense, command, i.e., present actions objectively as practically necessary; thus they are to be taken as counsels (*consilia*) rather than as commands (*praecepta*) of reason, and the task of determining infallibly and universally what action will promote the happiness of a rational being is completely unsolvable. There can be no imperative which would, in the strict sense, command us to do what makes for happiness, because happiness is an ideal not of reason but of imagination,[7] depending only on empirical grounds which one would expect in vain to determine an [419] action through which the totality of consequences—which is in fact infinite—could be achieved. Assuming that the means to happiness could be infallibly stated, this imperative of prudence would be an analytical proposition, for it differs from the imperative of skill only in that its end is given while in the latter case it is merely possible. Since both, however, only command the means to that which one presupposes, the imperative which commands the willing of the means to him who wills the end is in both cases analytical. There is, consequently, no difficulty in seeing the possibility of such an imperative.

To see how the imperative of morality is possible is, then,

---

[7] [The distinction between happiness and pleasure, which Kant says the followers of Epicurus confused, is explained in a fragment dating back to perhaps 1775: "Happiness is not something sensed but something thought. Nor is it a thought which can be taken from experience but a thought which only makes its experience possible. Not as if one had to know happiness in all its elements, but [one must know] the a priori condition by which alone one can be capable of happiness" (*Lose Blätter* [Reicke ed.], trans. Schilpp, in *Kant's Precritical Ethics*, p. 129).]

without doubt the only question needing an answer. It is not hypothetical, and thus the objectively conceived necessity cannot be supported by any presupposition, as was the case with the hypothetical imperatives. But it must not be overlooked that it cannot be shown by any example (i.e., it cannot be empirically shown) whether or not there is such an imperative; it is rather to be suspected that all imperatives which appear to be categorical may yet be hypothetical, but in a hidden way. For instance, when it is said, "Thou shalt not make a false promise," we assume that the necessity of this avoidance is not a mere counsel for the sake of escaping some other evil, so that it would read, "Thou shalt not make a false promise so that, if it comes to light, thou ruinest thy credit"; we assume rather that an action of this kind must be regarded as of itself bad and that the imperative of the prohibition is categorical. But we cannot show with certainty by any example that the will is here determined by the law alone without any other incentives, even though this appears to be the case. For it is always possible that secret fear of disgrace, and perhaps also obscure apprehension of other dangers, may have had an influence on the will. Who can prove by experience the nonexistence of a cause when experience shows us only that we do not perceive the cause? But in such a case the so-called moral imperative, which as such appears to be categorical and unconditional, would be actually only a pragmatic precept which makes us attentive to our own advantage and teaches us to consider it.

Thus we shall have to investigate purely a priori the possibility of a categorical imperative, for we do not have the [420] advantage that experience would give us the reality of this imperative, so that the [demonstration of its] possibility would be necessary only for its explanation and not for its establishment. In the meantime, this much may at least be seen: the categorical imperative alone can be taken as a practical *law*, while all the others may be called principles of the will but not laws. This is because what is necessary merely for the attainment of an arbitrary purpose can be regarded as itself contingent, and we get rid of the precept once we give up the purpose, whereas the unconditional command leaves the will no freedom to choose the opposite. Thus it alone implies the necessity which we require of a law.

Secondly, in the case of the categorical imperative or law of morality, the cause of difficulty in discerning its possibility is very weighty. This imperative is an a priori synthetical practical proposition,[8] and, since to discern the possibility of propositions of this sort is so difficult in theoretical knowledge, it may well be gathered that it will be no less difficult in the practical.

In attacking this problem, we will first inquire whether the mere concept of a categorical imperative does not also furnish the formula containing the proposition which alone can be a categorical imperative. For even when we know the formula of the imperative, to learn how such an absolute law is possible will require difficult and special labors which we shall postpone to the last section.

If I think of a hypothetical imperative as such, I do not know what it will contain until the condition is stated [under which it is an imperative]. But if I think of a categorical imperative, I know immediately what it contains. For since the imperative contains besides the law only the necessity [421] that the maxim[9] should accord with this law, while the law

[8] I connect a priori, and hence necessarily, the action with the will without supposing as a condition that there is any inclination [to the action] (though I do so only objectively, i.e., under the idea of a reason which would have complete power over all subjective motives). This is, therefore, a practical proposition which does not analytically derive the willing of an action from some other volition already presupposed (for we do not have such a perfect will); it rather connects it directly with the concept of the will of a rational being as something which is not contained within it.

[9] A maxim is the subjective principle of acting and must be distinguished from the objective principle, i.e., the practical law. The former contains the practical rule which reason determines according to the conditions of the subject (often its ignorance or inclinations) and is thus the principle according to which the subject acts. The law, on the other hand, is the objective principle valid for every rational being, and the principle by which it ought to act, i.e., an imperative.

contains no condition to which it is restricted, there is nothing remaining in it except the universality of law as such to which the maxim of the action should conform; and in effect this conformity alone is represented as necessary by the imperative.

There is, therefore, only one categorical imperative. It is: Act only according to that maxim by which you can at the same time will that it should become a universal law.

Now if all imperatives of duty can be derived from this one imperative as a principle, we can at least show what we understand by the concept of duty and what it means, even though it remain undecided whether that which is called duty is an empty concept or not.

The universality of law according to which effects are produced constitutes what is properly called nature in the most general sense (as to form), i.e., the existence of things so far as it is determined by universal laws. [By analogy], then, the universal imperative of duty can be expressed as follows: Act as though the maxim of your action were by your will to become a universal law of nature.

We shall now enumerate some duties, adopting the usual division of them into duties to ourselves and to others and into perfect and imperfect duties.[10]

1. A man who is reduced to despair by a series of evils feels a weariness with life but is still in possession of his reason [422] sufficiently to ask whether it would not be contrary to his duty to himself to take his own life. Now he asks whether the maxim of his action could become a universal law of nature. His maxim, however, is: For love of myself, I make it my principle to shorten my life when by a longer duration it

10 It must be noted here that I reserve the division of duties for a future *Metaphysics of Morals* and that the division here stands as only an arbitrary one (chosen in order to arrange my examples). For the rest, by a perfect duty I here understand a duty which permits no exception in the interest of inclination; thus I have not merely outer but also inner perfect duties. This runs contrary to the usage adopted in the schools, but I am not disposed to defend it here because it is all one to my purpose whether this is conceded or not.

threatens more evil than satisfaction. But it is questionable whether this principle of self-love could become a universal law of nature. One immediately sees a contradiction in a system of nature whose law would be to destroy life by the feeling whose special office is to impel the improvement of life. In this case it would not exist as nature; hence that maxim cannot obtain as a law of nature, and thus it wholly contradicts the supreme principle of all duty.

2. Another man finds himself forced by need to borrow money. He well knows that he will not be able to repay it, but he also sees that nothing will be loaned him if he does not firmly promise to repay it at a certain time. He desires to make such a promise, but he has enough conscience to ask himself whether it is not improper and opposed to duty to relieve his distress in such a way. Now, assuming he does decide to do so, the maxim of his action would be as follows: When I believe myself to be in need of money, I will borrow money and promise to repay it, although I know I shall never do so. Now this principle of self-love or of his own benefit may very well be compatible with his whole future welfare, but the question is whether it is right. He changes the pretension of self-love into a universal law and then puts the question: How would it be if my maxim became a universal law? He immediately sees that it could never hold as a universal law of nature and be consistent with itself; rather it must necessarily contradict itself. For the universality of a law which says that anyone who believes himself to be in need could promise what he pleased with the intention of not fulfilling it would make the promise itself and the end to be accomplished by it impossible; no one would believe what was promised to him but would only laugh at any such assertion as vain pretense.

3. A third finds in himself a talent which could, by means of some cultivation, make him in many respects a useful [423] man. But he finds himself in comfortable circumstances and prefers indulgence in pleasure to troubling himself with broadening and improving his fortunate natural gifts. Now, however, let him ask whether his maxim of neglecting his gifts,

besides agreeing with his propensity to idle amusement, agrees also with what is called duty. He sees that a system of nature could indeed exist in accordance with such a law, even though man (like the inhabitants of the South Sea Islands) should let his talents rust and resolve to devote his life merely to idleness, indulgence, and propagation—in a word, to pleasure. But he cannot possibly will that this should become a universal law of nature or that it should be implanted in us by a natural instinct. For, as a rational being, he necessarily wills that all his faculties should be developed, inasmuch as they are given to him for all sorts of possible purposes.

4. A fourth man, for whom things are going well, sees that others (whom he could help) have to struggle with great hardships, and he asks, "What concern of mine is it? Let each one be as happy as heaven wills, or as he can make himself; I will not take anything from him or even envy him; but to his welfare or to his assistance in time of need I have no desire to contribute." If such a way of thinking were a universal law of nature, certainly the human race could exist, and without doubt even better than in a state where everyone talks of sympathy and good will, or even exerts himself occasionally to practice them while, on the other hand, he cheats when he can and betrays or otherwise violates the rights of man. Now although it is possible that a universal law of nature according to that maxim could exist, it is nevertheless impossible to will that such a principle should hold everywhere as a law of nature. For a will which resolved this would conflict with itself, since instances can often arise in which he would need the love and sympathy of others, and in which he would have robbed himself, by such a law of nature springing from his own will, of all hope of the aid he desires.

The foregoing are a few of the many actual duties, or at least of duties we hold to be actual, whose derivation from the one stated principle is clear. We must be able to will that [424] a maxim of our action become a universal law; this is the canon of the moral estimation of our action generally. Some actions are of such a nature that their maxim cannot even be *thought* as a universal law of nature without contradiction, far from it being possible that one could will that it should be such. In others this internal impossibility is not found, though it is still impossible to *will* that their maxim should be raised to the universality of a law of nature, because such a will would contradict itself. We easily see that the former maxim conflicts with the stricter or narrower (imprescriptible) duty, the latter with broader (meritorious) duty. Thus all duties, so far as the kind of obligation (not the object of their action) is concerned, have been completely exhibited by these examples in their dependence on the one principle.

When we observe ourselves in any transgression of a duty, we find that we do not actually will that our maxim should become a universal law. That is impossible for us; rather, the contrary of this maxim should remain as a law generally, and we only take the liberty of making an exception to it for ourselves or for the sake of our inclination, and for this one occasion. Consequently, if we weighed everything from one and the same standpoint, namely, reason, we would come upon a contradiction in our own will, viz., that a certain principle is objectively necessary as a universal law and yet subjectively does not hold universally but rather admits exceptions. However, since we regard our action at one time from the point of view of a will wholly conformable to reason and then from that of a will affected by inclinations, there is actually no contradiction, but rather an opposition of inclination to the precept of reason (*antagonismus*). In this the universality of the principle (*universalitas*) is changed into mere generality (*generalitas*), whereby the practical principle of reason meets the maxim halfway. Although this cannot be justified in our own impartial judgment, it does show that we actually acknowledge the validity of the categorical imperative and allow ourselves (with all respect to it) only a few exceptions which seem to us to be unimportant and forced upon us.

We have thus at least established that if duty is a con- [425] cept which is to have significance and actual legislation for

our actions, it can be expressed only in categorical imperatives and not at all in hypothetical ones. For every application of it we have also clearly exhibited the content of the
categorical imperative which must contain the principle of all
duty (if there is such). This is itself very much. But we are
not yet advanced far enough to prove a priori that that kind
of imperative really exists, that there is a practical law which
of itself commands absolutely and without any incentives, and
that obedience to this law is duty.

With a view to attaining this, it is extremely important to
remember that we must not let ourselves think that the reality
of this principle can be derived from the particular constitution of human nature. For duty is practical unconditional
necessity of action; it must, therefore, hold for all rational beings (to which alone an imperative can apply), and only for
that reason can it be a law for all human wills. Whatever is
derived from the particular natural situation of man as such,
or from certain feelings and propensities, or even from a
particular tendency of the human reason which might not
hold necessarily for the will of every rational being (if such a
tendency is possible), can give a maxim valid for us but not a
law; that is, it can give a subjective principle by which we
might act only if we have the propensity and inclination, but
not an objective principle by which we would be directed to
act even if all our propensity, inclination, and natural tendency were opposed to it. This is so far the case that the sublimity and intrinsic worth of the command is the better shown
in a duty the fewer subjective causes there are for it and the
more there are against it; the latter do not weaken the constraint of the law or diminish its validity.

Here we see philosophy brought to what is, in fact, a precar-
ious position, which should be made fast even though it is
supported by nothing in either heaven or earth. Here philosophy must show its purity as the absolute sustainer of its laws,
and not as the herald of those which an implanted sense or
who knows what tutelary nature whispers to it. Those may be
better than no laws at all, but they can never afford funda-

mental principles, which reason alone dictates. These fundamental principles must originate entirely a priori and [426]
thereby obtain their commanding authority; they can expect
nothing from the inclination of men but everything from the
supremacy of the law and due respect for it. Otherwise they
condemn man to self-contempt and inner abhorrence.

Thus everything empirical is not only wholly unworthy to
be an ingredient in the principle of morality but is even
highly prejudicial to the purity of moral practices themselves.
For, in morals, the proper and inestimable worth of an absolutely good will consists precisely in the freedom of the
principle of action from all influences from contingent
grounds which only experience can furnish. We cannot too
much or too often warn against the lax or even base manner
of thought which seeks principles among empirical motives
and laws, for human reason in its weariness is glad to rest on
this pillow. In a dream of sweet illusions (in which it em-
braces not Juno but a cloud), it substitutes for morality a
bastard patched up from limbs of very different parentage,
which looks like anything one wishes to see in it, but not like
virtue to anyone who has ever beheld her in her true form.[11]

The question then is: Is it a necessary law for all rational
beings that they should always judge their actions by such
maxims as they themselves could will to serve as universal
laws? If it is such a law, it must be connected (wholly a priori)
with the concept of the will of a rational being as such. But
in order to discover this connection we must, however re-
luctantly, take a step into metaphysics, although into a region
of it different from speculative philosophy, i.e., into metaphysics of morals. In a practical philosophy it is not a question of
assuming grounds for what happens but of assuming laws of
what ought to happen even though it may never happen—

---

[11] To behold virtue in her proper form is nothing else than to exhibit
morality stripped of all admixture of sensuous things and of every spurious adornment of reward or self-love. How much she then eclipses everything which appears charming to the senses can easily be seen by everyone with the least effort of his reason, if it be not spoiled for all abstraction.

that is to say, objective, practical laws. Hence in practical philosophy we need not inquire into the reasons why [427] something pleases or displeases, how the pleasure of mere feeling differs from taste, and whether this is distinct from a general satisfaction of reason. Nor need we ask on what the feeling of pleasure or displeasure rests, how desires and inclinations arise, and how, finally, maxims arise from desires and inclination under the co-operation of reason. For all these matters belong to an empirical psychology, which would be the second part of physics if we consider it as philosophy of nature so far as it rests on empirical laws. But here it is a question of objectively practical laws and thus of the relation of a will to itself so far as it determines itself only by reason; for everything which has a relation to the empirical automatically falls away, because if reason of itself alone determines conduct it must necessarily do so a priori. The possibility of reason thus determining conduct must now be investigated.

The will is thought of as a faculty of determining itself to action in accordance with the conception of certain laws. Such a faculty can be found only in rational beings. That which serves the will as the objective ground of its self-determination is an end, and, if it is given by reason alone, it must hold alike for all rational beings. On the other hand, that which contains the ground of the possibility of the action, whose result is an end, is called the means. The subjective ground of desire is the incentive,[12] while the objective ground of volition is the motive. Thus arises the distinction between subjective ends, which rest on incentives, and objective ends, which depend on motives valid for every rational being. Practical principles are formal when they disregard all subjective ends; they are material when they have subjective ends, and thus certain incentives, as their basis. The ends which a rational being

12 [*Triebfeder* in contrast to *Bewegungsgrund*. Abbott translates the former as "spring," but "urge" might better convey the meaning. I follow Greene and Hudson's excellent usage in their translation of the *Religion Within the Limits of Reason Alone.*]

arbitrarily proposes to himself as consequences of his action are material ends and are without exception only relative, for only their relation to a particularly constituted faculty of desire in the subject gives them their worth. And this worth cannot, therefore, afford any universal principles for all rational beings or valid and necessary principles for every volition. That is, they cannot give rise to any practical laws. [428] All these relative ends, therefore, are grounds for hypothetical imperatives only.

But suppose that there were something the existence of which in itself had absolute worth, something which, as an end in itself, could be a ground of definite laws. In it and only in it could lie the ground of a possible categorical imperative, i.e., of a practical law.

Now, I say, man and, in general, every rational being exists as an end in himself and not merely as a means to be arbitrarily used by this or that will. In all his actions, whether they are directed to himself or to other rational beings, he must always be regarded at the same time as an end. All objects of inclinations have only a conditional worth, for if the inclinations and the needs founded on them did not exist, their object would be without worth. The inclinations themselves as the sources of needs, however, are so lacking in absolute worth that the universal wish of every rational being must be indeed to free himself completely from them. Therefore, the worth of any objects to be obtained by our actions is at all times conditional. Beings whose existence does not depend on our will but on nature, if they are not rational beings, have only a relative worth as means and are therefore called "things"; on the other hand, rational beings are designated "persons" because their nature indicates that they are ends in themselves, i.e., things which may not be used merely as means. Such a being is thus an object of respect and, so far, restricts all [arbitrary] choice. Such beings are not merely subjective ends whose existence as a result of our action has a worth for us, but are objective ends, i.e., beings whose existence in itself is an end. Such an end is one for which no other end can be substituted, to which these beings should serve merely as means. For, without them, nothing of absolute worth could be found, and if all worth is conditional and thus contingent, no supreme practical principle for reason could be found anywhere.

Thus if there is to be a supreme practical principle and a categorical imperative for the human will, it must be one that forms an objective principle of the will from the conception of that which is necessarily an end for everyone because it is an end in itself. Hence this objective principle can serve [429] as a universal practical law. The ground of this principle is: rational nature exists as an end in itself. Man necessarily thinks of his own existence in this way; thus far it is a subjective principle of human actions. Also every other rational being thinks of his existence by means of the same rational ground which holds also for myself;[13] thus it is at the same time an objective principle from which, as a supreme practical ground, it must be possible to derive all laws of the will. The practical imperative, therefore, is the following: Act so that you treat humanity, whether in your own person or in that of another, always as an end and never as a means only. Let us now see whether this can be achieved.

To return to our previous examples:

First, according to the concept of necessary duty to one's self, he who contemplates suicide will ask himself whether his action can be consistent with the idea of humanity as an end in itself. If, in order to escape from burdensome circumstances, he destroys himself, he uses a person merely as a means to maintain a tolerable condition up to the end of life. Man, however, is not a thing, and thus not something to be used merely as a means; he must always be regarded in all his actions as an end in himself. Therefore, I cannot dispose of man in my own person so as to mutilate, corrupt, or kill him. (It belongs to ethics proper to define more accurately this basic principle so as to avoid all misunderstanding, e.g., as to

---

[13] Here I present this proposition as a postulate, but in the last section grounds for it will be found.

the amputation of limbs in order to preserve myself, or to exposing my life to danger in order to save it; I must, therefore, omit them here.)

Second, as concerns necessary or obligatory duties to others, he who intends a deceitful promise to others sees immediately that he intends to use another man merely as a means, without the latter containing the end in himself at the same time. For he whom I want to use for my own purposes by means of such a promise cannot possibly assent to my mode of act- [430] ing against him and cannot contain the end of this action in himself. This conflict against the principle of other men is even clearer if we cite examples of attacks on their freedom and property. For then it is clear that he who transgresses the rights of men intends to make use of the persons of others merely as a means, without considering that, as rational beings, they must always be esteemed at the same time as ends, i.e., only as beings who must be able to contain in themselves the end of the very same action.[14]

Third, with regard to contingent (meritorious) duty to one's self, it is not sufficient that the action not conflict with humanity in our person as an end in itself; it must also harmonize with it. Now in humanity there are capacities for greater perfection which belong to the end of nature with respect to humanity in our own person; to neglect these might perhaps be consistent with the preservation of humanity as an end in itself but not with the furtherance of that end.

Fourth, with regard to meritorious duty to others, the natural end which all men have is their own happiness. Humanity might indeed exist if no one contributed to the hap-

---

[14] Let it not be thought that the banal *"quod tibi non vis fieri, etc.,"* could here serve as guide or principle, for it is only derived from the principle and is restricted by various limitations. It cannot be a universal law, because it contains the ground neither of duties to one's self nor of the benevolent duties to others (for many a man would gladly consent that others should not benefit him, provided only that he might be excused from showing benevolence to them). Nor does it contain the ground of obligatory duties to another, for the criminal would argue on this ground against the judge who sentences him. And so on.

piness of others, provided he did not intentionally detract from it; but this harmony with humanity as an end in itself is only negative rather than positive if everyone does not also endeavor, so far as he can, to further the ends of others. For the ends of any person, who is an end in himself, must as far as possible also be my end, if that conception of an end in itself is to have its full effect on me.

This principle of humanity and of every rational creature as an end in itself is the supreme limiting condition on [431] freedom of the actions of each man. It is not borrowed from experience, first, because of its universality, since it applies to all rational beings generally and experience does not suffice to determine anything about them; and, secondly, because in experience humanity is not thought of (subjectively) as the end of men, i.e., as an object which we of ourselves really make our end. Rather it is thought of as the objective end which should constitute the supreme limiting condition of all subjective ends, whatever they may be. Thus this principle must arise from pure reason. Objectively the ground of all practical legislation lies (according to the first principle) in the rule and in the form of universality, which makes it capable of being a law (at most a natural law); subjectively, it lies in the end. But the subject of all ends is every rational being as an end in itself (by the second principle); from this there follows the third practical principle of the will as the supreme condition of its harmony with universal practical reason, viz., the idea of the will of every rational being as making universal law.[15]

By this principle all maxims are rejected which are not consistent with the universal lawgiving of will. The will is thus not only subject to the law but subject in such a way that it must be regarded also as self-legislative and only for this reason as being subject to the law (of which it can regard itself as the author).

In the foregoing mode of conception, in which imperatives are conceived universally either as conformity to law by actions—a conformity which is similar to a natural order—

---

[15] [Following the suggestion of Paton, *The Categorical Imperative*, p. 180.]

or as the prerogative of rational beings as such, the imperatives exclude from their legislative authority all admixture
of any interest as an incentive. They do so because they were
conceived as categorical. They were only assumed to be categorical, however, because we had to make such an assumption
if we wished to explain the concept of duty. But that there
were practical propositions which commanded categorically
could not here be proved independently, just as little as it can
be proved anywhere in this section. One thing, however,
might have been done: to indicate in the imperative itself, by
some determination which it contained, that in volition [432]
from duty the renunciation of all interest is the specific mark
of the categorical imperative, distinguishing it from the hypothetical. And this is now being done in the third formulation
of the principle, i.e., in the idea of the will of every rational
being as a will giving universal law. A will which stands under
laws can be bound to this law by an interest. But if we think
of a will giving universal laws, we find that a supreme legislating will cannot possibly depend on any interest, for such a
dependent will would itself need still another law which would
restrict the interest of its self-love to the condition that [the
maxims of this will] should be valid as universal law.

Thus the principle of every human will as a will giving universal laws in all its maxims [16] is very well adapted to being a
categorical imperative, provided it is otherwise correct. Because of the idea of universal lawgiving, it is based on no
interest, and, thus of all possible imperatives, it alone can be
unconditional. Or, better, converting the proposition: if there
is a categorical imperative (a law for the will of every rational
being), it can only command that everything be done from the
maxim of its will as one which could have as its object only
itself considered as giving universal laws. For only in this case
are the practical principle and the imperative which the will

16 I may be excused from citing examples to elucidate this principle, for
those which have already illustrated the categorical imperative and its
formula can here serve the same purpose.

obeys unconditional, because the will can have no interest as its foundation.

If we now look back upon all previous attempts which have ever been undertaken to discover the principle of morality, it is not to be wondered at that they all had to fail. Man was seen to be bound to laws by his duty, but it was not seen that he is subject only to his own, yet universal, legislation, and that he is only bound to act in accordance with his own will, which is, however, designed by nature to be a will giving universal laws. For if one thought of him as subject only to a law (whatever it may be), this necessarily implied some in- [433] terest as a stimulus or compulsion to obedience because the law did not arise from his will. Rather, his will was constrained by something else according to a law to act in a certain way. By this strictly necessary consequence, however, all the labor of finding a supreme ground for duty was irrevocably lost, and one never arrived at duty but only at the necessity of action from a certain interest. This might be his own interest or that of another, but in either case the imperative always had to be conditional and could not at all serve as a moral command. This principle I will call the principle of *autonomy* of the will in contrast to all other principles which I accordingly count under *heteronomy*.

The concept of each rational being as a being that must regard itself as giving universal law through all the maxims of its will, so that it may judge itself and its actions from this standpoint, leads to a very fruitful concept, namely, that of a *realm of ends*.

By "realm" I understand the systematic union of different rational beings through common laws. Because laws determine ends with regard to their universal validity, if we abstract from the personal difference of rational beings and thus from all content of their private ends, we can think of a whole of all ends in systematic connection, a whole of rational beings as ends in themselves as well as of the particular ends which each may set for himself. This is a realm of ends, which is possible on the aforesaid principles. For all rational beings stand under the law that each of them should treat himself and all others never merely as means but in every case also as an end in himself. Thus there arises a systematic union of rational beings through common objective laws. This is a realm which may be called a realm of ends (certainly only an ideal), because what these laws have in view is just the relation of these beings to each other as ends and means.

A rational being belongs to the realm of ends as a [434] member when he gives universal laws in it while also himself subject to these laws. He belongs to it as sovereign when he, as legislating, is subject to the will of no other. The rational being must regard himself always as legislative in a realm of ends possible through the freedom of the will, whether he belongs to it as member or as sovereign. He cannot maintain the latter position merely through the maxims of his will but only when he is a completely independent being without need and with power adequate to his will.

Morality, therefore, consists in the relation of every action to that legislation through which alone a realm of ends is possible. This legislation, however, must be found in every rational being. It must be able to arise from his will, whose principle then is to take no action according to any maxim which would be inconsistent with its being a universal law and thus to act only so that the will through its maxims could regard itself at the same time as universally lawgiving. If now the maxims do not by their nature already necessarily conform to this objective principle of rational beings as universally lawgiving, the necessity of acting according to that principle is called practical constraint, i.e., duty. Duty pertains not to the sovereign in the realm of ends, but rather to each member, and to each in the same degree.

The practical necessity of acting according to this principle, i.e., duty, does not rest at all on feelings, impulses, and inclinations; it rests merely on the relation of rational beings to one another, in which the will of a rational being must always be regarded as legislative, for otherwise it could not be thought of as an end in itself. Reason, therefore, relates every maxim of the will as giving universal laws to every other will and also to every action toward itself; it does so not for the sake of any other practical motive or future advantage but rather from the idea of the dignity of a rational being who obeys no law except that which he himself also gives.

In the realm of ends everything has either a *price* or a *dignity*. Whatever has a price can be replaced by something else as its equivalent; on the other hand, whatever is above all price, and therefore admits of no equivalent, has a dignity.

That which is related to general human inclinations and needs has a *market price*. That which, without presupposing any need, accords with a certain taste, i.e., with pleasure [435] in the mere purposeless play of our faculties, has an *affective price*. But that which constitutes the condition under which alone something can be an end in itself does not have mere relative worth, i.e., a price, but an intrinsic worth, i.e., *dignity*.

Now morality is the condition under which alone a rational being can be an end in itself, because only through it is it possible to be a legislative member in the realm of ends. Thus morality and humanity, so far as it is capable of morality, alone have dignity. Skill and diligence in work have a market value; wit, lively imagination, and humor have an affective price; but fidelity in promises and benevolence on principle (not from instinct) have intrinsic worth. Nature and likewise art contain nothing which could replace their lack, for their worth consists not in effects which flow from them, nor in advantage and utility which they procure; it consists only in intentions, i.e., maxims of the will which are ready to reveal themselves in this manner through actions even though success does not favor them. These actions need no recommendation from any subjective disposition or taste in order that they may be looked upon with immediate favor and satisfaction, nor do they have need of any immediate propensity or feeling directed to them. They exhibit the will which performs them as the object of an immediate respect, since nothing but reason is required in order to impose them on the will. The will is not to be cajoled into them, for this, in the case of duties, would be a contradiction. This esteem lets the worth of such a turn of mind be recognized as dignity and puts it infinitely beyond any price, with which it cannot in the least be brought into competition or comparison without, as it were, violating its holiness.

And what is it that justifies the morally good disposition or virtue in making such lofty claims? It is nothing less than the participation it affords the rational being in giving universal laws. He is thus fitted to be a member in a possible realm of ends to which his own nature already destined him. For, as an end in himself, he is destined to be legislative in the realm of ends, free from all laws of nature and obedient only to those which he himself gives. Accordingly, his maxims can be- [436] long to a universal legislation to which he is at the same time also subject. A thing has no worth other than that determined for it by the law. The legislation which determines all worth must therefore have a dignity, i.e., unconditional and incomparable worth. For the esteem which a rational being must have for it, only the word "respect" is a suitable expression. Autonomy is thus the basis of the dignity of both human nature and every rational nature.

The three aforementioned ways of presenting the principle of morality are fundamentally only so many formulas of the very same law, and each of them unites the others in itself. There is, nevertheless, a difference in them, but the difference is more subjectively than objectively practical, for it is intended to bring an idea of reason closer to intuition (by means of a certain analogy) and thus nearer to feeling. All maxims have:

1. A form, which consists in universality; and in this respect the formula of the moral imperative requires that the maxims be chosen as though they should hold as universal laws of nature.

2. A material, i.e., an end; in this respect the formula says that the rational being, as by its nature an end and thus as an

end in itself, must serve in every maxim as the condition restricting all merely relative and arbitrary ends.

3. A complete determination of all maxims by the formula
that all maxims which stem from autonomous legislation
ought to harmonize with a possible realm of ends as with a
realm of nature.[17]

There is a progression here like that through the categories
of the unity of the form of the will (its universality), the
plurality of material (the objects, i.e., the ends), and the all-
comprehensiveness or totality of the system of ends. But it is
better in moral evaluation to follow the rigorous method and
to make the universal formula of the categorical imperative
the basis: Act according to the maxim which can at the [437]
same time make itself a universal law. But if one wishes to
gain a hearing for the moral law, it is very useful to bring one
and the same action under the three stated principles and
thus, so far as possible, to bring it nearer to intuition.

We can now end where we started, with the concept of an
unconditionally good will. That will is absolutely good which
cannot be bad, and thus it is a will whose maxim, when made
a universal law, can never conflict with itself. Thus this principle is also its supreme law: Always act according to that
maxim whose universality as a law you can at the same time
will. This is the only condition under which a will can never
come into conflict with itself, and such an imperative is categorical. Because the validity of the will, as a universal law
for possible actions, has an analogy with the universal connection of the existence of things under universal laws, which
is the formal element of nature in general, the categorical
imperative can also be expressed as follows: Act according to

---

17 Teleology considers nature as a realm of ends; morals regards a possible realm of ends as a realm of nature. In the former the realm of ends
is a theoretical idea for the explanation of what actually is. In the latter
it is a practical idea for bringing about that which is not actually real but
which can become real through our conduct, and which is in accordance
with this idea.

maxims which can at the same time have themselves as universal laws of nature as their object. Such, then, is the formula of an absolutely good will.

Rational nature is distinguished from others in that it proposes an end to itself. This end would be the material of every good will. Since, however, in the idea of an absolutely good will without any limiting condition of the attainment of this or that end, every end to be effected must be completely abstracted (as any particular end would make each will only relatively good), the end here is not conceived as one to be effected but as an independent end, and thus merely negatively. It is that which must never be acted against, and which must consequently never be valued as merely a means but in every volition also as an end. Now this end can never be other than the subject of all possible ends themselves, because this is at the same time the subject of a possible will which is absolutely good; for the latter cannot be made secondary to any other object without contradiction. The principle: Act with reference to every rational being (whether yourself or another) so that it is an end in itself in your maxim, is thus basically [438] identical with the principle: Act by a maxim which involves its own universal validity for every rational being.

That in the use of means to every end I should restrict my maxim to the condition of its universal validity as a law for every subject is tantamount to saying that the subject of ends, i.e., the rational being itself, must be made the basis of all maxims of actions and must thus be treated never as a mere means but as the supreme limiting condition in the use of all means, i.e., as an end at the same time.

It follows incontestably that every rational being must be able to regard himself as an end in himself with reference to all laws to which he may be subject, whatever they may be, and thus as giving universal laws. For it is just the fitness of his maxims to a universal legislation that indicates that he is an end in himself. It also follows that his dignity (his prerogative) over all merely natural beings entails that he must take his maxims from the point of view which regards himself, and hence also every other rational being, as legislative. (The rational beings are, on this account, called persons.) In this way, a world of rational beings (*mundus intelligibilis*) is possible as a realm of ends, because of the legislation belonging to all persons as members. Consequently, every rational being must act as if he, by his maxims, were at all times a legislative member in the universal realm of ends. The formal principle of these maxims is: So act as if your maxims should serve at the same time as the universal law (of all rational beings). A realm of ends is thus possible only by analogy with a realm of nature. The former, however, is possible only by maxims, i.e., self-imposed rules, while the latter is possible by laws of efficient causes of things externally necessitated. Regardless of this difference, by analogy we call the natural whole a realm of nature so far as it is related to rational beings as its end; we do so even though the natural whole is looked at as a machine. Such a realm of ends would actually be realized through maxims whose rule is prescribed to all rational beings by the categorical imperative, if they were universally obeyed. But a rational being, though he scrupulously follow this maxim, cannot for that reason expect every other rational being to be true to it; nor can he expect the realm of nature and its orderly design to harmonize with him as a fitting member of a realm of ends which is possible through himself. That is, he cannot count on its favoring his expectation of hap- [439] piness. Still the law: Act according to the maxims of a universally legislative member of a merely potential realm of ends, remains in full force, because it commands categorically. And just in this lies the paradox that merely the dignity of humanity as rational nature without any end or advantage to be gained by it, and thus respect for a mere idea, should serve as the inflexible precept of the will. There is the further paradox that the sublimity of the maxims and the worthiness of every rational subject to be a legislative member in the realm of ends consist precisely in independence of the maxims from all such incentives. Otherwise he would have to be viewed as subject only to the natural law of his needs. Although the realm of nature as well as that of ends would be thought of as united under a sovereign so that the latter would no longer remain a mere idea but would receive true reality, the realm of ends would undoubtedly gain a strong urge in its favor, but its intrinsic worth would not be augmented. Regardless of this, even the one and only absolute legislator would still have to be conceived as judging the worth of rational beings only by the disinterested conduct which they prescribe to themselves merely from the idea [of dignity]. The essence of things is not changed by their external relations, and without reference to these relations a man must be judged only by what constitutes his absolute worth; and this is true whoever his judge is, even if it be the Supreme Being. Morality is thus the relation of actions to the autonomy of the will, i.e., to possible universal lawgiving by maxims of the will. The action which can be compatible with the autonomy of the will is permitted; that which does not agree with it is prohibited. The will whose maxims necessarily are in harmony with the laws of autonomy is a holy will or an absolutely good will. The dependence of a will not absolutely good on the principle of autonomy (moral constraint) is *obligation*. Hence obligation cannot be applied to a holy will. The objective necessity of an action from obligation is called *duty*.

From what has just been said, it can easily be explained how it happens that, although in the concept of duty we think of subjection to law, we do nevertheless ascribe a certain sublimity and dignity to the person who fulfills all his [440] duties. For though there is no sublimity in him in so far as he is subject to the moral law, yet he is sublime in so far as he is legislative with reference to the law and subject to it only for this reason. We have also shown above how neither fear of nor inclination to the law is the incentive which can give a moral worth to action; only respect for it can do so. Our own will, so far as it would act only under the condition of a universal legislation rendered possible by its maxims—this will, ideally possible for us, is the proper object of respect, and the dignity of humanity consists just in its capacity of giving universal laws, although with the condition that it is itself subject to this same legislation.

### THE AUTONOMY OF THE WILL AS THE SUPREME PRINCIPLE OF MORALITY

Autonomy of the will is that property of it by which it is a law to itself independently of any property of objects of volition. Hence the principle of autonomy is: Never choose except in such a way that the maxims of the choice are comprehended in the same volition as a universal law. That this practical rule is an imperative, that is, that the will of every rational being is necessarily bound to it as a condition, cannot be proved by a mere analysis of the concepts occurring in it, because it is a synthetical proposition. To prove it, we would have to go beyond the knowledge of objects to a critical examination of the subject, i.e., of the pure practical reason, for this synthetical proposition which commands apodictically must be susceptible of being known completely a priori. This matter, however, does not belong in the present section. But that the principle of autonomy, which is now in question, is the sole principle of morals can be readily shown by mere analysis of concepts of morality; for by this analysis we find that its principle must be a categorical imperative and that the imperative commands neither more nor less than this very autonomy.

### THE HETERONOMY OF THE WILL AS THE SOURCE OF ALL SPURIOUS PRINCIPLES OF MORALITY

If the will seeks the law which is to determine it any- [441] where else than in the fitness of its maxims to its own universal legislation, and if it thus goes outside itself and seeks this law in the property of any of its objects, heteronomy always results. For then the will does not give itself the law, but the object through its relation to the will gives the law to it. This relation, whether it rests on inclination or on conceptions of reason, only admits of hypothetical imperatives: I should do something for the reason that I will something else. The moral, and therewith categorical, imperative, on the other hand, says I should act this or that way even though I will nothing else. For example, the former says I should not lie if I wish to keep my reputation. The latter says I should not lie even though it would not cause me the least injury. The latter, therefore, must disregard every object to such an extent that it has absolutely no influence on the will, so that practical reason (will) may not merely minister to an interest not its own but rather may show its commanding authority as the supreme legislation. Thus, for instance, I should seek to further the happiness of others, not as though its realization was any concern of mine (whether because of direct inclination or of some satisfaction related to it indirectly through reason); I should do so merely because the maxim which excludes it from my duty cannot be comprehended as a universal law in one and the same volition.

## CLASSIFICATION OF ALL POSSIBLE PRINCIPLES OF MORALITY FOLLOWING FROM THE ASSUMED PRINCIPLE OF HETERONOMY

Here as everywhere in the pure use of reason, so long as a critical examination of it is lacking, human reason at first tries all possible wrong ways before it succeeds in finding the one true way.

All principles which can be taken in this point of view are either empirical or rational. The former, drawn from the principle of happiness, are based on physical or moral [442] feeling; the latter, drawn from the principle of perfection, are based either on the rational concept of perfection as a possible result or on the concept of an independent perfection (the will of God) as the determining cause of our will.

Empirical principles are not at all suited to serve as the basis of moral laws. For if the basis of the universality by which they should be valid for all rational beings without distinction (the unconditional practical necessity which is thereby imposed upon them) is derived from a particular tendency of human nature or the accidental circumstance in which it is found, that universality is lost. But the principle of one's own happiness is the most objectionable of all. This is not merely because it is false and because experience contradicts the supposition that well-being is always proportional to good conduct, nor yet because this principle contributes nothing to the establishment of morality, inasmuch as it is a very different thing to make a man happy from making him good, and to make him prudent and farsighted for his own advantage is far from making him virtuous. Rather, it is because this principle supports morality with incentives which undermine it and destroy all its sublimity, for it puts the motives to virtue and those to vice in the same class, teaching us only to make a better calculation while obliterating the specific difference between them. On the other hand, there is the alleged special sense,[18] the moral feeling. The appeal to it is superficial, since those who cannot think expect help from feeling, even with respect to that which concerns universal laws; they do so even though feelings naturally differ so infinitely in degree that they are incapable of furnishing a uniform standard of the good and bad, and also in spite of the fact that one cannot validly judge for others by means of his own feeling. Nevertheless, the moral feeling is nearer to morality and its dignity, inasmuch as it pays virtue the honor of ascribing the satisfaction and esteem for her directly to morality, and does not, as it were, say to her face that it is not her beauty but only [443] our advantage which attaches us to her.

Among the rational principles of morality, there is the ontological concept of perfection. It is empty, indefinite, and consequently useless for finding in the immeasurable field of

---

[18] I count the principle of moral feeling under that of happiness, because every empirical interest promises to contribute to our well-being by the agreeableness that a thing affords, either directly and without a view to future advantage or with a view to it. We must likewise, with Hutcheson, count the principle of sympathy with the happiness of others under the moral sense which he assumed.

possible reality the greatest possible sum which is suitable to us; and, in specifically distinguishing the reality which is here in question from all other reality, it inevitably tends to move in a circle and cannot avoid tacitly presupposing the morality which it ought to explain. Nevertheless, it is better than the theological concept, which derives morality from a most perfect divine will. It is better not merely because we cannot intuit its perfection, having rather to derive it only from our own concepts of which morality itself is foremost, but also because if we do not so derive it (and to do so would involve a most flagrant circle in explanation), the only remaining concept of the divine will is made up of the attributes of desire for glory and dominion combined with the awful conceptions of might and vengeance, and any system of ethics based on them would be directly opposed to morality.

But if I had to choose between the concept of the moral sense and that of perfection in general (neither of which at any rate weakens morality, although they are not capable of serving as its foundations), I would decide for the latter, because it preserves the indefinite idea (of a will good in itself) free from corruption until it can be more narrowly defined. It at least withdraws the decision of the question from sensibility and brings it to the court of pure reason, although it does not even here decide the question.

For the rest, I think that I may be excused from a lengthy refutation of all these doctrines. It is so easy, and presumably so well understood even by those whose office requires them to decide for one of these theories (since the hearers would not tolerate suspension of judgment), that such a refutation would be only superfluous work. What interests us more, however, is to know that all these principles set up nothing other than the heteronomy of the will as the first ground of morality and thus necessarily miss their aim.

In every case in which an object of the will must be [444] assumed as prescribing the rule which is to determine the will, the rule is nothing else but heteronomy. The imperative in this case is conditional, stating that if or because one wills this object, one should act thus or so. Therefore the imperative can never command morally, that is, categorically. The object may determine the will by means of inclination, as in the principle of one's own happiness, or by means of reason directed to objects of our possible volition in general, as in the principle of perfection; but the will in these cases never determines itself directly by the conception of the action itself but only by the incentive which the foreseen result of the action incites in the will—that is, "I ought to do something because I will something else." And here still another law must be assumed in my person as the basis of this imperative; it would be a law by which I would necessarily will that other thing; but this law would again require an imperative to restrict this maxim. Since the conception of an object commensurate to our power incites in the will an impulse according to the natural characteristic of our person, this impulse belongs to the nature of the subject (either to the sensibility, i.e., inclination and taste, or to understanding and reason, which faculties, according to the particular constitution of their nature, take pleasure in exercising themselves on an object). It follows that it would be really nature that would give the law. As a law of nature, known and proved by experience, it would be contingent and therefore unfit to be an apodictical practical rule such as the moral rule must be. Such a law always represents heteronomy of the will; the will does not give itself the law, but an external impulse gives it to the will according to the nature of the subject which is adapted to receive it.

The absolutely good will, the principle of which must be a categorical imperative, is thus undetermined with reference to any objects. It contains only the form of volition in general, and this form is autonomy. That is, the capability of the maxims of every good will to make themselves universal laws is itself the sole law which the will of every rational being imposes on itself, and it does not need to support this on any incentive or interest.

How such a synthetical practical a priori proposition is possible and why it is necessary is a problem whose solution does not lie within the boundaries of the metaphysics of morals. Moreover, we have not here affirmed its truth, and even [445] less professed to command a proof of it. We showed only through the development of the universally received concept of morals that autonomy of the will is unavoidably connected with it, or rather that it is its foundation. Whoever, therefore. holds morality to be something real and not a chimerical idea without truth must also concede its principle which has been adduced here. Consequently, this section was merely analytical, like the first. To prove that morality is not a mere phantom of the mind—and if the categorical imperative, and with it the autonomy of the will, is true and absolutely necessary as an a priori principle, it follows that it is no phantom—requires that a synthetical use of pure practical reason is possible. But we must not venture on this use without first making a critical examination of this faculty of reason. In the last section we shall give the principal features of such an examination that will be sufficient for our purpose.

## THIRD SECTION

## TRANSITION FROM THE METAPHYSICS OF MORALS TO THE CRITICAL EXAMINATION OF PURE PRACTICAL REASON

### THE CONCEPT OF FREEDOM IS THE KEY TO THE EXPLANATION OF THE AUTONOMY OF THE WILL

As will is a kind of causality of living beings so far as [446] they are rational, freedom would be that property of this causality by which it can be effective independently of foreign causes determining it, just as natural necessity is the property of the causality of all irrational beings by which they are determined in their activity by the influence of foreign causes.

The preceding definition of freedom is negative and therefore affords no insight into its essence. But a positive concept of freedom flows from it which is so much the richer and more fruitful. Since the concept of a causality entails that of laws according to which something, i.e., the effect, must be established through something else which we call cause, it follows that freedom is by no means lawless even though it is not a property of the will according to laws of nature. Rather, it must be a causality according to immutable laws, but of a peculiar kind. Otherwise a free will would be an absurdity. Natural necessity is, as we have seen, a heteronomy of efficient causes, for every effect is possible only according to the law that something else determines the efficient cause to its causality. What else, then, can the freedom of the will be but [447] autonomy, i.e., the property of the will to be a law to itself? The proposition that the will is a law to itself in all its actions, however, only expresses the principle that we should act according to no other maxim than that which can also have itself as a universal law for its object. And this is just the formula of the categorical imperative and the principle of morality. Therefore a free will and a will under moral laws are identical.

Thus if freedom of the will is presupposed, morality together with its principle follows from it by the mere analysis of its concept. But the principle is nevertheless a synthetical proposition: an absolutely good will is one whose maxim can always include itself as a universal law. It is synthetical because by analysis of the concept of an absolutely good will that property of the maxim cannot be found. Such synthetical propositions, however, are possible only by the fact that both cognitions are connected through their union with a third in which both of them are to be found. The positive concept of freedom furnishes this third cognition, which cannot be, as in the case of physical causes, the nature of the sensuous world, in the concept of which we find conjoined the concepts of something as cause in relation to something else as effect. We cannot yet show directly what this third cognition is to which freedom directs us and of which we have an a priori idea, nor can we explain the deduction of the concept of freedom from

pure practical reason and therewith the possibility of a categorical imperative. For this some further preparation is
needed.

## FREEDOM MUST BE PRESUPPOSED AS THE PROPERTY OF THE WILL OF ALL RATIONAL BEINGS

It is not enough to ascribe freedom to our will, on any
grounds whatever, if we do not also have sufficient grounds for
attributing it to all rational beings. For since morality serves
as a law for us only as rational beings, morality must hold
valid for all rational beings, and since it must be derived exclusively from the property of freedom, freedom as the property of the will of all rational beings must be demonstrated.
And it does not suffice to prove it from certain alleged [448]
experiences of human nature (which is indeed impossible, as
it can be proved only a priori), but we must prove it as belonging generally to the activity of rational beings endowed
with a will. Now I say that every being which cannot act otherwise than under the idea of freedom is thereby really free
in a practical respect. That is to say, all laws which are inseparably bound up with freedom hold for it just as if its will
were proved free in itself by theoretical philosophy.[1] Now I
affirm that we must necessarily grant that every rational being
who has a will also has the idea of freedom and that it acts
only under this idea. For in such a being we think of a reason
which is practical, i.e., a reason which has causality with respect to its objects. Now, we cannot conceive of a reason which
consciously responds to a bidding from the outside with respect to its judgments, for then the subject would attribute

---

[1] I follow this method, assuming that it is sufficient for our purpose that
rational beings take merely the idea of [in der Idee] freedom as basic to
their actions, in order to avoid having also to prove freedom in its theoretical aspect. For if the latter is left unproved, the laws which would
obligate a being who was really free would hold for a being who cannot
act except under the idea of his own freedom. Thus we can escape here
from the onus which presses on the theory.

the determination of its power of judgment not to reason but to an impulse. Reason must regard itself as the author of its principles, independently of foreign influences; consequently, as practical reason or as the will of a rational being, it must regard itself as free. That is to say, the will of a rational being can be a will of its own only under the idea of freedom, and therefore in a practical point of view such a will must be ascribed to all rational beings.

### OF THE INTEREST ATTACHING TO THE IDEAS OF MORALITY

We have finally reduced the definite concept of morality to the idea of freedom, but we could not prove freedom to be real in ourselves and in human nature. We saw only that [449] we must presuppose it if we would think of a being as rational and conscious of his causality with respect to actions, that is, as endowed with a will; and so we find that on the very same grounds we must ascribe to each being endowed with reason and will the property of determining himself to action under the idea of freedom.

From presupposing this idea [of freedom] there followed also consciousness of a law of action: that the subjective principles of actions, i.e., maxims, in every instance must be so chosen that they can hold also as objective, i.e., universal, principles, and thus can serve as principles for the universal laws we give. But why should I subject myself as a rational being, and thereby all other beings endowed with reason, to this law? I will admit that no interest impels me to do so, for that would then give no categorical imperative. But I must nevertheless take an interest in it and see how it comes about, for this "ought" is properly a "would" that is valid for every rational being provided reason is practical for him without hindrance [i.e., exclusively determines his action]. For beings who like ourselves are affected by the senses as incentives different from reason and who do not always do that which reason for itself alone would have done, that necessity of action is expressed only as an "ought." The subjective necessity is thus distinguished from the objective.

It therefore seems that the moral law, i.e., the principle of the autonomy of the will, is, properly speaking, only presupposed in the idea of freedom, as if we could not prove its reality and objective necessity by itself. Even if that were so, we would still have gained something because we would at least have defined the genuine principle more accurately than had been done before. But with regard to its validity and to the practical necessity of subjection to it, we would not have advanced a single step, for we could give no satisfactory answer to anyone who asked us why the universal validity of our maxim as of a law had to be the restricting condition of our action. We could not tell on what is based the worth we ascribe to actions of this kind—a worth so great that there can be no higher interest, nor could we tell how it happens that man believes it is only through this that he feels his own personal worth, in contrast to which the worth of a [450] pleasant or unpleasant condition is to be regarded as nothing.

We do find sometimes that we can take an interest in a personal quality which involves no [personal] interest in any [external] condition, provided only that [possession of] this quality makes us capable of participating in the [desired] condition in case reason were to effect the allotment of it. That is, mere worthiness to be happy even without the motive of participating in it can interest us of itself. But this judgment is in fact only the effect of the already assumed importance of moral laws (if by the idea of freedom we detach ourselves from every empirical interest). But that we ought to detach ourselves, i.e., regard ourselves as free in acting and yet as subject to certain laws, in order to find a worth merely in our person which would compensate for the loss of everything which makes our situation desirable—how this is possible and hence on what grounds the moral law obligates us we still cannot see in this way.

We must openly confess that there is a kind of circle here from which it seems that there is no escape. We assume that

we are free in the order of efficient causes so that we can conceive of ourselves as subject to moral laws in the order of
ends. And then we think of ourselves as subject to these laws
because we have ascribed freedom of the will to ourselves.
This is circular because freedom and self-legislation of the will
are both autonomy and thus are reciprocal concepts, and for
that reason one of them cannot be used to explain the other
and to furnish a ground for it. At most they can be used for
the logical purpose of bringing apparently different conceptions of the same object under a single concept (as we reduce
different fractions of the same value to the lowest common
terms).

One recourse, however, remains open to us, namely, to inquire whether we do not assume a different standpoint when
we think of ourselves as causes a priori efficient through freedom from that which we occupy when we conceive of ourselves in the light of our actions as effects which we see before
our eyes.

The following remark requires no subtle reflection, and we
may suppose that even the commonest understanding can
make it, though it does so, after its fashion, by an ob- [451]
scure discernment of judgment which it calls feeling: all conceptions, like those of the senses, which come to us without
our choice enable us to know the objects only as they affect
us, while what they are in themselves remains unknown to us;
therefore, as regards this kind of conception, even with the
closest attention and clearness which understanding may ever
bring to them we can attain only to knowledge of appearances
and never to knowledge of things in themselves. As soon as
this distinction is made (perhaps merely because of a difference noticed between conceptions which are given to us from
somewhere else and to which we are passive and those which
we produce only from ourselves and in which we show our
own activity), it follows of itself that we must admit and
assume behind the appearances something else which is not
appearance, namely, things in themselves; we do so although
we must admit that we cannot approach them more closely

and can never know what they are in themselves, since they can never be known by us except as they affect us. This must furnish a distinction, though a crude one, between a world of sense and a world of understanding. The former, by differences in the sensuous faculties, can be very different among various observers, while the latter, which is its foundation, remains always the same. A man may not presume to know even himself as he really is by knowing himself through inner sensation. For since he does not, as it were, produce himself or derive his concept of himself a priori but only empirically, it is natural that he obtains his knowledge of himself through inner sense and consequently only through the appearance of his nature and the way in which his consciousness is affected. But beyond the characteristic of his own subject which is compounded of these mere appearances, he necessarily assumes something else as its basis, namely, his ego as it is in itself. Thus in respect to mere perception and receptivity to sensations he must count himself as belonging to the world of sense; but in respect to that which may be pure activity in himself (i.e., in respect to that which reaches consciousness directly and not by affecting the senses) he must reckon himself as belonging to the intellectual world. But he has no further knowledge of that world.

To such a conclusion the thinking man must come with respect to all things which may present themselves to [452] him. Presumably it is to be met with in the commonest understanding which, as is well known, is very much inclined to expect behind the objects of the senses something else invisible and acting of itself. But such an understanding soon spoils it by trying to make the invisible again sensuous, i.e., to make it an object of intuition. Thus common understanding becomes not in the least wiser.

Now man really finds in himself a faculty by which he distinguishes himself from all other things, even from himself so far as he is affected by objects. This faculty is reason. As a pure spontaneous activity it is elevated even above understanding. For though the latter is also a spontaneous activity and does not, like sense, merely contain conceptions which arise only when one is affected by things, being passive, it nevertheless cannot produce by its activity any other concepts than those which serve to bring the sensuous conceptions under rules, and thereby to unite them in one consciousness. Without this use of sensibility it would not think at all, while, on the other hand, reason shows such a pure spontaneity in the case of ideas that it [2] far transcends everything that sensibility can give to consciousness and shows its chief occupation in distinguishing the world of sense from the world of understanding, thereby prescribing limits to the understanding itself.

For this reason a rational being must regard himself as intelligence (and not from the side of his lower powers), as belonging to the world of understanding and not to that of the senses. Thus he has two standpoints from which he can consider himself and recognize the laws of the employment of his powers and consequently of all his actions: first, as belonging to the world of sense under laws of nature (heteronomy), and, second, as belonging to the intelligible world under laws which, independent of nature, are not empirical but founded only on reason.

As a rational being and thus as belonging to the intelligible world, man cannot think of the causality of his own will except under the idea of freedom, for independence from the determining causes of the world of sense (an independence which reason must always ascribe to itself) is freedom. The concept of autonomy is inseparably connected with the idea of freedom, and with the former there is inseparably bound the universal principle of morality, which ideally is the ground of all actions of rational beings, just as natural law is the [453] ground of all appearances.

Now we have removed the suspicion which we raised that there might be a hidden circle in our reasoning from freedom

2 [Kant wrote *er* . . . . *ihm,* which gives no tenable meaning. Adickes suggested *sie* . . . . *ihr = reason* . . . . *to reason.* But as sensibility does not give material to reason, at least directly, Vorländer and the Cassirer ed. read *sie* . . . . *ihm,* and they are followed here.]

to autonomy and from the latter to the moral law. This suspicion was that we laid down the idea of freedom for the sake
of the moral law in order later to derive the latter from freedom, and that we were thus unable to give any ground for the
law, presenting it only as a *petitio principii* that well-disposed
minds would gladly allow us but which we could never advance as a demonstrable proposition. But we now see that, if
we think of ourselves as free, we transport ourselves into the
intelligible world as members of it and know the autonomy of
the will together with its consequence, morality; while, if we
think of ourselves as obligated, we consider ourselves as belonging both to the world of sense and at the same time to
the intelligible world.

## HOW IS A CATEGORICAL IMPERATIVE POSSIBLE?

The rational being counts himself, qua intelligence, as belonging to the intelligible world, and only as an efficient
cause belonging to it does he call his causality a will. On the
other side, however, he is conscious of himself as a part of the
world of sense in which his actions are found as mere appearances of that causality. But we do not discern how they are
possible on the basis of that causality which we do not know;
rather, those actions must be regarded as determined by other
appearances, namely, desires and inclinations, belonging to
the world of sense. As a mere member of the intelligible
world, all my actions would completely accord with the principle of the autonomy of the pure will, and as a part only of
the world of sense would they have to be assumed to conform
wholly to the natural law of desires and inclinations and thus
to the heteronomy of nature. (The former actions would rest
on the supreme principle of morality, and the latter on that of
happiness.) But since the intelligible world contains the
ground of the world of sense and hence of its laws, the intelligible world is (and must be conceived as) directly legislative
for my will, which belongs wholly to the intelligible world.
Therefore I recognize myself qua intelligence as subject [454]

to the law of the world of understanding and to the autonomy of the will. That is, I recognize myself as subject to the law of reason which contains in the idea of freedom the law of the intelligible world, while at the same time I must acknowledge that I am a being which belongs to the world of sense. Therefore I must regard the laws of the intelligible world as imperatives for me, and actions in accord with this principle as duties.

Thus categorical imperatives are possible because the idea of freedom makes me a member of an intelligible world. Consequently, if I were a member of only that world, all my actions *would* always be in accordance with the autonomy of the will. But since I intuit myself at the same time as a member of the world of sense, my actions *ought* to conform to it, and this categorical ought presents a synthetic a priori proposition, since besides my will affected by my sensuous desires there is added the idea of exactly the same will as pure, practical of itself, and belonging to the intelligible world, which according to reason contains the supreme condition of the former [sensuously affected] will. It is similar to the manner in which concepts of the understanding, which of themselves mean nothing but lawful form in general, are added to the intuitions of the sensuous world, thus rendering possible a priori synthetic propositions on which all knowledge of a system of nature rests.

The practical use of common human reason confirms the correctness of this deduction. When we present examples of honesty of purpose, of steadfastness in following good maxims, and of sympathy and general benevolence even with great sacrifice of advantages and comfort, there is no man, not even the most malicious villain (provided he is otherwise accustomed to using his reason), who does not wish that he also might have these qualities. But because of his inclinations and impulses he cannot bring this about, yet at the same time he wishes to be free from such inclinations which are burdensome even to himself. He thus proves that, with a will free from all impulses of sensibility, he in thought transfers himself into an order of things altogether different from that of his desires in the field of sensibility. He cannot expect to obtain by that wish any gratification of desires or any condition which would satisfy his real or even imagined inclinations, for the idea itself, which elicits this wish from him, would lose its pre-eminence if he had any such expectation. He can expect only a greater inner worth of his person. He imagines himself to be this better person when he transfers him- [455] self to the standpoint of a member of the intelligible world to which he is involuntarily impelled by the idea of freedom, i.e., independence from the determining causes of the world of sense; and from this standpoint he is conscious of a good will, which on his own confession constitutes the law for his bad will as a member of the world of sense. He acknowledges the authority of this law even while transgressing it. The moral ought is therefore his own volition as a member of the intelligible world, and it is conceived by him as an ought only in so far as he regards himself at the same time as a member of the world of sense.

### ON THE EXTREME LIMIT OF ALL PRACTICAL PHILOSOPHY

In respect to their will, all men think of themselves as free. Hence arise all judgments of actions as being such as ought to have been done, although they were not done. But this freedom is not an empirical concept and cannot be such, for it still remains even though experience shows the contrary of the demands which are necessarily conceived as consequences of the supposition of freedom. On the other hand, it is equally necessary that everything which happens should be inexorably determined by natural laws, and this natural necessity is likewise no empirical concept, because it implies the concept of necessity and thus of a priori knowledge. But this concept of a system of nature is confirmed by experience, and it is inevitably presupposed if experience, which is knowledge of the objects of the senses interconnected by universal laws, is to be possible. Therefore freedom is only an idea of reason whose objective reality in itself is doubtful, while nature is a concept of the understanding which shows and necessarily must show its reality by examples in experience.

There now arises a dialectic of reason, since the freedom ascribed to the will seems to stand in contradiction to natural necessity. At this parting of the ways reason in its speculative purpose finds the way of natural necessity more well-beaten and usable than that of freedom; but in its practical purpose the footpath of freedom is the only one on which it is [456] possible to make use of reason in our conduct. Hence it is as impossible for the subtlest philosophy as for the commonest reasoning to argue freedom away. Philosophy must therefore assume that no true contradiction will be found between freedom and natural necessity in the same human actions, for it cannot give up the concept of nature any more than that of freedom.

Hence even if we should never be able to conceive how freedom is possible, at least this apparent contradiction must be convincingly eradicated. For if even the thought of freedom contradicts itself or nature, which is equally necessary, it would have to be surrendered in competition with natural necessity.

But it would be impossible to escape this contradiction if the subject, who seems to himself free, thought of himself in the same sense or in the same relationship when he calls himself free as when he assumes that in the same action he is subject to natural law. Therefore it is an inescapable task of speculative philosophy to show at least that its illusion about the contradiction rests in the fact that we [do not] [3] think of man in a different sense and relationship when we call him free from that in which we consider him as a part of nature and subject to its laws. It must show not only that they can very well coexist but also that they must be thought of as necessarily united in one and the same subject; for otherwise no ground could be given why we should burden reason with

[3] [Following the suggestion of R. F. A. Hoernlé, *Mind*, XLV (new ser., 1936), 127-28.]

an idea which, though it may without contradiction be united with another that is sufficiently established, nevertheless involves us in a perplexity which sorely embarrasses reason in its speculative use. This duty is imposed only on speculative philosophy, so that it may clear the way for practical philosophy. Thus the philosopher has no choice as to whether he will remove the apparent contradiction or leave it untouched, for in the latter case the theory of it would be *bonum vacans*, into the possession of which the fatalist can rightly enter and drive all morality from its alleged property as occupying it without title.

Yet we cannot say here that we have reached the beginnings of practical philosophy. For the settlement of the controversy does not belong to practical philosophy, as the latter demands from speculative reason only that it put an end to the [457] discord in which it entangles itself in theoretical questions, so that practical reason may have rest and security from outer attacks which could dispute with it the ground on which it desires to erect its edifice.

The title to freedom of the will claimed by common reason is based on the consciousness and the conceded presupposition of the independence of reason from merely subjectively determining causes which together constitute what belongs only to sensation, being comprehended under the general name of sensibility. Man, who in this way regards himself as intelligence, puts himself in a different order of things and in a relationship to determining grounds of an altogether different kind when he thinks of himself as intelligence with a will and thus as endowed with causality, compared with that other order of things and that other set of determining grounds which become relevant when he perceives himself as a phenomenon in the world of sense (as he really also is) and submits his causality to external determination according to natural laws. Now he soon realizes that both can subsist together—indeed, that they must. For there is not the least contradiction between a thing in appearance (as belonging to the world of sense) being subject to certain laws of which it is independent as a thing or a being in itself. That it must think of itself in this twofold manner rests, with regard to the first, on the consciousness of itself as an object affected through the senses, and, with regard to what is required by the second, on the consciousness of itself as intelligence, i.e., as independent of sensuous impressions in the use of reason and thus as belonging to the intelligible world.

This is why man claims to possess a will which does not let him become accountable for what belongs merely to his desires and inclinations, but thinks of actions which can be performed only by disregarding all desires and sensuous attractions, as possible and indeed necessary for him. The causality of these actions lies in him as an intelligence and in effects and actions in accordance with principles of an intelligible world, of which he knows only that reason alone and indeed pure reason independent of sensibility gives the law in it. Moreover, since it is only as intelligence that he is his proper self (being as man only appearance of himself), he knows that those laws apply to him directly and categorically, so that that to which inclinations and impulses and hence the entire nature of the world of sense incite him cannot in the least impair the laws of his volition as an intelligence. He does not even hold himself responsible for these inclinations and impulses or attrib- [458] ute them to his proper self, i.e., his will, though he does ascribe to his will the indulgence which he may grant to them when he permits them an influence on his maxims to the detriment of the rational laws of his will.

When practical reason thinks itself into an intelligible world, it does in no way transcend its limits. It would do so, however, if it tried to intuit or feel itself into it. The intelligible world is only a negative thought with respect to the world of sense, which does not give reason any laws for determining the will. It is positive only in the single point that freedom as negative determination is at the same time connected with a positive faculty and even a causality of reason. This causality we call a will to act so that the principle of actions will accord with the essential characteristic of a rational cause, i.e., with the condition of the universal validity of a maxim as a law. But if it were to borrow an object of the will, i.e., a motive, from the intelligible world, it would overstep its boundaries and pretend to be acquainted with something of which it knows nothing. The concept of a world of understanding is therefore only a standpoint which reason sees itself forced to take outside of appearances, in order to think of itself as practical. If the influences of sensibility were determining for man, this would not be possible; but it is necessary unless he is to be denied the consciousness of himself as an intelligence, and thus as a rational and rationally active cause, i.e., a cause acting in freedom. This thought certainly implies the idea of an order and legislation different from that of natural mechanism which applies to the world of sense; and it makes necessary the concept of an intelligible world, the whole of rational beings as things in themselves. But it does not give us the least occasion to think of it otherwise than according to its formal condition only, i.e., the universality of the maxim of the will as law and thus the autonomy of the will, which alone is consistent with freedom. All laws, on the other hand, which are directed to an object make for heteronomy, which belongs only to natural laws and which can apply only to the world of sense.

But reason would overstep all its bounds if it undertook to explain how pure reason can be practical, which is the [459] same problem as explaining how freedom is possible.

For we can explain nothing but what we can reduce to laws whose object can be given in some possible experience. But freedom is a mere idea, the objective reality of which can in no way be shown according to natural laws or in any possible experience. Since no example in accordance with any analogy can support it, it can never be comprehended or even imagined. It holds only as the necessary presupposition of reason in a being that believes itself conscious of a will, i.e., of a faculty different from the mere faculty of desire, or a faculty of determining itself to act as intelligence and thus according to laws of reason independently of natural instincts. But where determination according to natural laws comes to an end, there too all explanation ceases and nothing remains but defense, i.e., refutation of the objections of those who pretend to have seen more deeply into the essence of things and therefore boldly declare freedom to be impossible. We can only show them that the supposed contradiction they have discovered lies nowhere else than in their necessarily regarding man as appearance in order to make natural law valid with respect to human actions. And now when we require them to think of him qua intelligence as a thing in itself, they still persist in considering him as appearance. Obviously, then, the separation of his causality (his will) from all natural laws of the world of sense in one and the same subject is a contradiction, but this disappears when they reconsider and confess, as is reasonable, that behind the appearances things in themselves must stand as their hidden ground and that we cannot expect the laws of the activity of these grounds to be the same as those under which their appearances stand.

The subjective impossibility of explaining the freedom of the will is the same as the impossibility of discovering and explaining an interest [4] which man can take in moral laws. [460] Nevertheless, he does actually take an interest in them, and the foundation in us of this interest we call the moral feeling. This moral feeling has been erroneously construed by some as

[4] Interest is that by which reason becomes practical, i.e., a cause determining the will. We therefore say only of a rational being that he takes an interest in something; irrational creatures feel only sensuous impulses. A direct interest in the action is taken by reason only if the universal validity of its maxim is a sufficient determining ground of the will. Only such an interest is pure. But if reason can determine the will only by means of another object of desire or under the presupposition of a particular feeling of the subject, reason takes merely an indirect interest in the action, and since reason by itself alone without experience can discover neither objects of the will nor a particular feeling which lies at its root, that indirect interest would be only empirical and not a pure interest of reason. The logical interest of reason in advancing its insights is never direct but rather presupposes purposes for which they are to be used.

the standard for our moral judgment, whereas it must rather be regarded as the subjective effect which the law has upon the will to which reason alone gives objective grounds.

In order to will that which reason alone prescribes to the sensuously affected rational being as that which he ought to will, certainly there is required a power of reason to instill a feeling of pleasure or satisfaction in the fulfillment of duty, and hence there must be a causality of reason to determine the sensibility in accordance with its own principles. But it is wholly impossible to discern, i.e., to make a priori conceivable, how a mere thought containing nothing sensuous is to produce a sensation of pleasure or displeasure. For that is a particular kind of causality of which, as of all causality, we cannot determine anything a priori but must consult experience only. But since experience can exemplify the relation of cause to effect only as subsisting between two objects of experience, while here pure reason by mere Ideas (which furnish no object for experience) is to be the cause of an effect which does lie in experience, an explanation of how and why the universality of the maxim as law (and hence morality) interests us is completely impossible for us men. Only this much is certain: that it is valid for us not because it interests us (for that is heteronomy and dependence of practical reason on sensibility, i.e., on a basic feeling, and thus it could never be morally [461] legislative), but that it interests us because it is valid for us as men, inasmuch as it has arisen from our will as intelligence and hence from our proper self; but what belongs to mere appearance is necessarily subordinated by reason to the nature of the thing in itself.

Thus the question, "How is a categorical imperative possible?" can be answered to this extent: We can cite the only presupposition under which it is alone possible. This is the Idea of freedom, and we can discern the necessity of this presupposition which is sufficient to the practical use of reason, i.e., to the conviction of the validity of this imperative and hence also of the moral law. But how this presupposition itself is possible can never be discerned by any human reason. However, on the presupposition of freedom of the will of an intelligence, its autonomy as the formal condition under which alone it can be determined is a necessary consequence. To presuppose the freedom of the will is not only quite possible, as speculative philosophy itself can prove, for it does not involve itself in a contradiction with the principle of natural necessity in the interconnection of appearances in the world of sense. But it is also unconditionally necessary that a rational being conscious of his causality through reason and thus conscious of a will different from desires should practically presuppose it, i.e., presuppose it in the idea as the fundamental condition of all his voluntary actions. Yet how pure reason, without any other incentives, wherever they may be derived, can by itself be practical, i.e., how the mere principle of the universal validity of all its maxims as laws (which would certainly be the form of a pure practical reason), without any material (object) of the will in which we might in advance take some interest, can itself furnish an incentive and produce an interest which would be called purely moral; or, in other words, how pure reason can be practical—to explain this, all human reason is wholly incompetent, and all the pains and work of seeking an explanation of it are wasted.

It is just the same as if I sought to find out how freedom itself as causality of a will is possible; for, in so doing, I [462] would leave the philosophical basis of explanation behind, and I have no other. Certainly I could revel in the intelligible world, the world of intelligences, which still remains to me; but although I have a well-founded idea of it, still I do not have the least knowledge of it, nor can I ever attain to it by all the exertions of my natural capacity of reason. This intelligible world signifies only a something which remains when I have excluded from the determining grounds of my will everything. belonging to the world of sense in order to withhold the principle of motives from the field of sensibility. I do so by limiting it and showing that it does not contain absolutely everything in itself but that outside it there is still more; but this more I do not further know. After banishing all material, i.e., knowledge of objects, from pure reason which formulates this ideal, there remain to me only the form, the practical law of universal validity of maxims, and, in conformity with this, reason in relation to a pure intelligible world as a possible effective cause, i.e., as determining the will. An incentive must here be wholly absent unless this idea of an intelligible world itself be the incentive or that in which reason primarily takes an interest. But to make this conceivable is precisely the problem we cannot solve.

Here is, then, the supreme limit of all moral inquiry. To define it is very important, both in order that reason may not seek around, on the one hand, in the world of sense, in a way harmful to morals, for the supreme motive and for a comprehensible but empirical interest; and so that it will not, on the other hand, impotently flap its wings in the space (for it, an empty space) of transcendent concepts which we call the intelligible world, without being able to move from its starting point, or lose itself amid phantoms. Furthermore, the idea of a pure intelligible world as a whole of all intelligences to which we ourselves belong as rational beings (though on the other side we are at the same time members of the world of sense) is always a useful and permissible idea for the purpose of a rational faith. This is so even though all knowledge terminates at its boundary, for through the glorious ideal of a universal realm of ends-in-themselves (rational beings) a lively interest in the moral law can be awakened in us. To that realm we can belong as members only when we carefully [463] conduct ourselves according to maxims of freedom as if they were laws of nature.

### CONCLUDING REMARK

The speculative use of reason with respect to nature leads to the absolute necessity of some supreme cause of the world. The practical use of reason with respect to freedom leads also to an absolute necessity, but to the necessity only of laws of actions of a rational being as such. Now it is an essential prin-

ciple of all use of reason to push its knowledge to a consciousness of its necessity, for otherwise it would not be rational
knowledge. But it is also an equally essential restriction of
this very same reason that it cannot discern the necessity of
what is or what occurs or what ought to be done, unless a condition under which it is or occurs or ought to be done is presupposed. In this way, however, the satisfaction of reason is
only further and further postponed by the constant inquiry
after the condition. Therefore, reason restlessly seeks the unconditionally necessary and sees itself compelled to assume it,
though it has no means by which to make it comprehensible
and is happy enough if it can only discover the concept which
is consistent with this presupposition. It is therefore no objection to our deduction of the supreme principle of morality,
but a reproach which we must make to human reason generally, that it cannot render comprehensible the absolute necessity of an unconditional practical law (such as the categorical
imperative must be). Reason cannot be blamed for being un-
willing to explain it by a condition, i.e., by making some interest its basis, for the law would then cease to be moral, i.e.,
a supreme law of freedom. And so we do not indeed comprehend the practical unconditional necessity of the moral imperative; yet we do comprehend its incomprehensibility, which
is all that can be fairly demanded of a philosophy which in its
principles strives to reach the limit of human reason.

## II

# WHAT IS ENLIGHTENMENT?

Enlightenment is man's release from his self-incurred tute-lage. Tutelage is man's inability to make use of his understanding without direction from another. Self-incurred is this tutelage when its cause lies not in lack of reason but in lack of resolution and courage to use it without direction from another. *Sapere aude!* [1] "Have courage to use your own reason!"—that is the motto of enlightenment.

Laziness and cowardice are the reasons why so great a portion of mankind, after nature has long since discharged them from external direction (*naturaliter maiorennes*), nevertheless remains under lifelong tutelage, and why it is so easy for others to set themselves up as their guardians. It is so easy not to be of age. If I have a book which understands for me, a pastor who has a conscience for me, a physician who decides my diet, and so forth, I need not trouble myself. I need not think, if I can only pay—others will readily undertake the irksome work for me.

That the step to competence is held to be very dangerous by the far greater portion of mankind (and by the entire fair sex) —quite apart from its being arduous—is seen to by those guardians who have so kindly assumed superintendence over them. After the guardians have first made their domestic cattle dumb and have made sure that these placid creatures will not dare take a single step without the harness of the cart to which they are tethered, the guardians then show them the danger which threatens if they try to go alone. Actually, however, this danger is not so great, for by falling a few times they would

---

[1] ["Dare to know!" (Horace *Ars poetica*). This was the motto adopted in 1736 by the Society of the Friends of Truth, an important circle in the German Enlightenment.]

finally learn to walk alone. But an example of this failure makes them timid and ordinarily frightens them away from all further trials.

For any single individual to work himself out of the life under tutelage which has become almost his nature is very difficult. He has come to be fond of this state, and he is for the present really incapable of making use of his reason, for no one has ever let him try it out. Statutes and formulas, those mechanical tools of the rational employment or rather misemployment of his natural gifts, are the fetters of an everlasting tutelage. Whoever throws them off makes only an uncertain leap over the narrowest ditch because he is not accustomed to that kind of free motion. Therefore, there are few who have succeeded by their own exercise of mind both in freeing themselves from incompetence and in achieving a steady pace.

But that the public should enlighten itself is more possible; indeed, if only freedom is granted, enlightenment is almost sure to follow. For there will always be some independent thinkers, even among the established guardians of the great masses, who, after throwing off the yoke of tutelage from their own shoulders, will disseminate the spirit of the rational appreciation of both their own worth and every man's vocation for thinking for himself. But be it noted that the public, which has first been brought under this yoke by their guardians, forces the guardians themselves to remain bound when it is incited to do so by some of the guardians who are themselves capable of some enlightenment—so harmful is it to implant prejudices, for they later take vengeance on their cultivators or on their descendants. Thus the public can only slowly attain enlightenment. Perhaps a fall of personal despotism or of avaricious or tyrannical oppression may be accomplished by revolution, but never a true reform in ways of thinking. Rather, new prejudices will serve as well as old ones to harness the great unthinking masses.

For this enlightenment, however, nothing is required but freedom, and indeed the most harmless among all the things to which this term can properly be applied. It is the freedom to make public use of one's reason at every point.[2] But I hear on all sides, "Do not argue!" The officer says: "Do not argue but drill!" The tax collector: "Do not argue but pay!" The cleric: "Do not argue but believe!" Only one prince in the world says, "Argue as much as you will, and about what you will, but obey!" Everywhere there is restriction on freedom.

Which restriction is an obstacle to enlightenment, and which is not an obstacle but a promoter of it? I answer: The public use of one's reason must always be free, and it alone can bring about enlightenment among men. The private use of reason, on the other hand, may often be very narrowly restricted without particularly hindering the progress of enlightenment. By the public use of one's reason I understand the use which a person makes of it as a scholar before the reading public. Private use I call that which one may make of it in a particular civil post or office which is entrusted to him. Many affairs which are conducted in the interest of the community require a certain mechanism through which some members of the community must passively conduct themselves with an artificial unanimity, so that the government may direct them to public ends, or at least prevent them from destroying those ends. Here argument is certainly not allowed—one must obey. But so far as a part of the mechanism regards himself at the same time as a member of the whole community or of a society of world citizens, and thus in the role of a scholar who addresses the public (in the proper sense of the word) through his writings, he certainly can argue without hurting the affairs for which he is in part responsible as a passive member. Thus it would be ruinous for an officer in service to debate about the suitability or utility of a command given to him by his superior; he must obey. But the right to make remarks on errors in the military service and to lay them before the public for judgment cannot equitably be refused him as a scholar. The citizen cannot refuse to pay the taxes

2 [It is this freedom Kant claimed later in his conflict with the censor, deferring to the censor in the "private" use of reason, i.e., in his lectures.]

imposed on him; indeed, an impudent complaint at those
levied on him can be punished as a scandal (as it could
occasion general refractoriness). But the same person nevertheless does not act contrary to his duty as a citizen when, as a
scholar, he publicly expresses his thoughts on the inappropri-
ateness or even the injustice of these levies. Similarly a clergyman is obligated to make his sermon to his pupils in catechism
and his congregation conform to the symbol of the church
which he serves, for he has been accepted on this condition.
But as a scholar he has complete freedom, even the calling, to
communicate to the public all his carefully tested and well-
meaning thoughts on that which is erroneous in the symbol
and to make suggestions for the better organization of the
religious body and church. In doing this there is nothing that
could be laid as a burden on his conscience. For what he
teaches as a consequence of his office as a representative of the
church, this he considers something about which he has no
freedom to teach according to his own lights; it is something
which he is appointed to propound at the dictation of and in
the name of another. He will say, "Our church teaches this or
that; those are the proofs which it adduces." He thus extracts
all practical uses for his congregation from statutes to which
he himself would not subscribe with full conviction but to the
enunciation of which he can very well pledge himself because
it is not impossible that truth lies hidden in them, and, in any
case, there is at least nothing in them contradictory to inner
religion. For if he believed he had found such in them, he
could not conscientiously discharge the duties of his office; he
would have to give it up. The use, therefore, which an appointed teacher makes of his reason before his congregation
is merely private, because this congregation is only a domestic
one (even if it be a large gathering); with respect to it, as a
priest, he is not free, nor can he be free, because he carries
out the orders of another. But as a scholar, whose writings
speak to his public, the world, the clergyman in the public use
of his reason enjoys an unlimited freedom to use his own reason and to speak in his own person. That the guardians of the

people (in spiritual things) should themselves be incompetent is an absurdity which amounts to the eternalization of absurdities.

But would not a society of clergymen, perhaps a church conference or a venerable classis (as they call themselves among the Dutch), be justified in obligating itself by oath to a certain unchangeable symbol in order to enjoy an unceasing guardianship over each of its members and thereby over the people as a whole, and even to make it eternal? I answer that this is altogether impossible. Such a contract, made to shut off all further enlightenment from the human race, is absolutely null and void even if confirmed by the supreme power, by parliaments, and by the most ceremonious of peace treaties. An age cannot bind itself and ordain to put the succeeding one into such a condition that it cannot extend its (at best very occasional) knowledge, purify itself of errors, and progress in general enlightenment. That would be a crime against human nature, the proper destination of which lies precisely in this progress; and the descendants would be fully justified in rejecting those decrees as having been made in an unwarranted and malicious manner.

The touchstone of everything that can be concluded as a law for a people lies in the question whether the people could have imposed such a law on itself. Now such a religious compact might be possible for a short and definitely limited time, as it were, in expectation of a better. One might let every citizen, and especially the clergyman, in the role of scholar, make his comments freely and publicly, i.e., through writing, on the erroneous aspects of the present institution. The newly introduced order might last until insight into the nature of these things had become so general and widely approved that through uniting their voices (even if not unanimously) they could bring a proposal to the throne to take those congregations under protection which had united into a changed religious organization according to their better ideas, without, however, hindering others who wish to remain in the order. But to unite in a permanent religious institution which is not to be subject to doubt before the public even in the lifetime of one man, and thereby to make a period of time fruitless in the progress of mankind toward improvement, thus working to the disadvantage of posterity—that is absolutely forbidden. For himself (and only for a short time) a man may postpone enlightenment in what he ought to know, but to renounce it for himself and even more to renounce it for posterity is to injure and trample on the rights of mankind.

And what a people may not decree for itself can even less be decreed for them by a monarch, for his lawgiving authority rests on his uniting the general public will in his own. If he only sees to it that all true or alleged improvement stands together with civil order, he can leave it to his subjects to do what they find necessary for their spiritual welfare. This is not his concern, though it is incumbent on him to prevent one of them from violently hindering another in determining and promoting this welfare to the best of his ability. To meddle in these matters lowers his own majesty, since by the writings in which his subjects seek to present their views he may evaluate his own governance. He can do this when, with deepest understanding, he lays upon himself the reproach, *Caesar non est supra grammaticos.* Far more does he injure his own majesty when he degrades his supreme power by supporting the ecclesiastical despotism of some tyrants in his state over his other subjects.

If we are asked, "Do we now live in an *enlightened age?*" the answer is, "No," but we do live in an *age of enlightenment.*[3] As things now stand, much is lacking which prevents men from being, or easily becoming, capable of correctly using their own reason in religious matters with assurance and free from outside direction. But, on the other hand, we have clear indications that the field has now been opened wherein men may freely deal with these things and that the obstacles to general enlightenment or the release from self-imposed tute-

[3] ["Our age is, in especial degree, the age of criticism, and to criticism everything must submit" (*Critique of Pure Reason,* Preface to first ed. [Smith trans.]).]

lage are gradually being reduced. In this respect, this is the age of enlightenment, or the century of Frederick.

A prince who does not find it unworthy of himself to say that he holds it to be his duty to prescribe nothing to men in religious matters but to give them complete freedom while renouncing the haughty name of *tolerance,* is himself enlightened and deserves to be esteemed by the grateful world and posterity as the first, at least from the side of government, who divested the human race of its tutelage and left each man free to make use of his reason in matters of conscience. Under him venerable ecclesiastics are allowed, in the role of scholars, and without infringing on their official duties, freely to submit for public testing their judgments and views which here and there diverge from the established symbol. And an even greater freedom is enjoyed by those who are restricted by no official duties. This spirit of freedom spreads beyond this land, even to those in which it must struggle with external obstacles erected by a government which misunderstands its own interest. For an example gives evidence to such a government that in freedom there is not the least cause for concern about public peace and the stability of the community. Men work themselves gradually out of barbarity if only intentional artifices are not made to hold them in it.

I have placed the main point of enlightenment—the escape of men from their self-incurred tutelage—chiefly in matters of religion because our rulers have no interest in playing the guardian with respect to the arts and sciences and also because religious incompetence is not only the most harmful but also the most degrading of all. But the manner of thinking of the head of a state who favors religious enlightenment goes further, and he sees that there is no danger to his lawgiving in allowing his subjects to make public use of their reason and to publish their thoughts on a better formulation of his legislation and even their open-minded criticisms of the laws already made. Of this we have a shining example wherein no monarch is superior to him whom we honor.

But only one who is himself enlightened, is not afraid of

shadows, and has a numerous and well-disciplined army to assure public peace, can say: "Argue as much as you will, and about what you will, only obey!" A republic could not dare say such a thing. Here is shown a strange and unexpected trend in human affairs in which almost everything, looked at in the large, is paradoxical. A greater degree of civil freedom appears advantageous to the freedom of mind of the people, and yet it places inescapable limitations upon it; a lower degree of civil freedom, on the contrary, provides the mind with room for each man to extend himself to his full capacity. As nature has uncovered from under this hard shell the seed for which she most tenderly cares—the propensity and vocation to free thinking—this gradually works back upon the character of the people, who thereby gradually become capable of managing freedom; finally, it affects the principles of government, which finds it to its advantage to treat men, who are now more than machines, in accordance with their dignity.[4]

I. KANT

KÖNIGSBERG, PRUSSIA
September 30, 1784

4 Today I read in the *Büschingsche Wöchentliche Nachrichten* for September 13 an announcement of the *Berlinische Monatsschrift* for this month, which cites the answer to the same question by Herr Mendelssohn.* But this issue has not yet come to me; if it had, I would have held back the present essay, which is now put forth only in order to see how much agreement in thought can be brought about by chance.

  * [Mendelssohn's answer was that enlightenment lay in intellectual cultivation, which he distinguished from the practical. Kant, quite in line with his later essay on theory and practice, refuses to make this distinction fundamental.]